The Disappearance of Julie Weflen

Ruth Kanton

Published by Trellis Publishing, 2021.

THE DISAPPEARANCE OF JULIE WEFLEN

First edition. July 12, 2021.

ISBN: 979-8224306732

Written by Ruth Kanton.

THE DISAPPEARANCE OF JULIE ANN WEFLEN

RUTH CANTON

Julie Ann Miner Weflen
1957 - 1980

Julie Ann Miner was born on May 3, 1957, to Robert E. and Bette Miner. There isn't much information regarding Julie's childhood. Julie had an older sister named Robin, and they grew up with their parents in Portland Oregon. She attended the Beaumont Grade School, and went on to graduate from Grant High School in 1977. By all accounts, Julie was a good student, and she never found herself in trouble with law enforcement as she was growing up.

Julie had dark hair and dark eyes, and was usually quick to smile. She was a strong child, and was able to keep a positive outlook even after she was diagnosed with scoliosis as a teenager. Most people who met her marveled at the straight, perfect posture she had, with some even assuming that she was a kindergarten teacher. After her diagnosis, Julie had to undergo surgery to help straighten out her spine. The surgery went well, and Julie left with a steel rod inserted into her spine to correct the curvature. During the recovery period, Julie spent six months in a cast. The cast covered the greater part of her upper body, going all the way from her hips to just under her chin. She finally made a full recovery, and graduated from high school with good grades.

Julie's career choice baffled many, especially since she was considered beautiful and looked more like a school teacher than anything else. In 1977, after she graduated, she started working at the Bonneville Power Administration, which was known to many as BPA. She wasn't interested in the desk jobs, and chose instead to become a power station operator. She was 18 years old at the time. No one ever understood why she chose what was considered at the time as a "man's job" but Julie was content. She was a hard worker, and was able to withstand the hazing and pranks that her male colleagues planned against her. However, Julie had bigger plans in mind, and being an operator was not all she wanted to do. When an opening for a safety officer came about at the company, she was more than ready to apply for it. She was a good candidate, but lacked the proper qualifications for the position. Her superiors saw her potential, but they were convinced that it was a man's job. Julie was the only female applicant out of the six that wanted the job, and the company executives were worried she wouldn't make it.

The safety officer job required that the person holding that position would be responsible for the lives of the employees who worked as linemen and were always up on the poles. This meant automatically figuring out which lines to use when rerouting the power in case a lineman was working on a power supply shortage. The officer was also supposed to immediately figure out which switches needed to be switched off in order to prevent a widespread power blackout. These two roles were of the greatest importance, as any mistakes would have serious repercussions for the employee and the company. As it turned out, Julie was not scared by the daunting task ahead of her. She maintained that she still wanted the promotion, and enrolled in the BPA rigorous training program set out for the applicants.

For the next three years, Julie kept up with her 40-hour work weeks, and added the training to her schedule. Every six months, Julie undertook twenty lessons, and made a point of mastering every single one of them. She had to take tests, and she sent the results to Bonneville for assessment after she was done. This wasn't the only requirement. After the written tests, she also had to take oral tests that were meant to assess the candidate's knowledge. The program also required that candidates memorize complex electrical formulas, which made it even more challenging. She worked tenaciously, and she made sure that every test taken was a sure pass. She did not let herself down. Throughout this period, Julie was taunted and teased by her male colleagues, and the hazing did not stop. She took it all in stride, and soon after, they realized that she was serious and more than capable of handling the job's challenges. The teasing and jokes turned into new found respect and admiration.

At the end of the program, Julie proved to her superiors that the safety officer job could be done by women. She was one of the two candidates who got the promotion. Her hard work had paid off.

Mike Weflen

Mike Weflen was attending a jazz concert in Portland when he laid his eyes on Julie. The 26-year-old was a troubleshooter for a condominium developer. He was a ladies man, and with his blondish brown hair and slate-blue eyes, it wasn't that hard to figure out why. The handsome young man was five years older than Julie at the time. That 1980 jazz concert changed Mike's life forever. In an interview with Ann Rule, author of *Kiss Me, Kill Me and Other True Cases,* Mike told her that on that first day, he immediately knew that Julie was special. "You can just sense a kind of comfort when you meet some people," he told Rule.

The two had a good time getting to know each other during the concert. That evening, Mike asked Julie out on a date. The 21-year-old was delighted to say yes. The connection between the two had been strong for both of them. After the date, Mike and Julie began dating, and were together ever since. Mike's parents were delighted that their son had met someone nice, and were looking forward to meeting her. Mike's mother, Phyllis Weflen even said, "The best description of Julie is that she radiates love." Mike's parents liked Julie, and were happy that the two were doing so well.

Mike and Julie both enjoyed the outdoors, and their free time was spent on one thing or the other. Mike was particularly fond of skiing, and Julie was a great horse lover, and preferred horseback riding. They made time for each other's activities, and Mike even promised to get Julie a horse one day. Mike said, "You know, we really didn't have any particular common interests; we just got along." The relationship was quiet and relaxed, but it had its fair share of fights and disagreements.

After dating for three years, the two tied the knot on June 25, 1983. On her part, Julie was having successes both in her personal and professional life, and she seemed perfectly content. After living in Portland for a year and half as a married couple, the two decided to make a serious change. They packed up and moved to the Seattle area. By this time, Mike had also switched careers, and was a commercial painter. In a time when women were mostly stay-at-home wives, Mike seemed to be as open-minded as Julie. He never asked her to quit her job, even though they had spoken about how getting children would change the relationship dynamics.

So when Julie was offered yet another promotion by Bonneville Power Administration, Mike was quick to encourage her to take it. The new promotion meant that Mike and Julie had to move again, this time to Spokane County, to the east of Cascade Mountains, near the Idaho border. It seemed like a big leap moving from a big city to a rural town, but the two were actually excited about it. Mike had been born and raised in South Dakota, and was used to the slow and quiet pace of country life that wasn't available in Seattle. Julie was an Oregon girl, and she shared the same sentiments with her husband. While Mike's business was solely based in Seattle, he figured there would be no harm in opening his business in Spokane also.

Once they got to Spokane, the two settled into their life with a commitment unlike any other. For Mike, making sure Julie was okay was his biggest concern, and he did everything in his power to always be there to protect her. One of his biggest sacrifices was deciding to take up work as a painter, which he did primarily to ensure that his schedule would be able to match up with Julie's. Her work was scheduled on a shift basis, which made her worry that they were not spending enough free time as a couple. With Mike's flexible schedule, the time constraints on their relationship quickly became a thing of the past. In Spokane, Julie was first posted indoors, and she worked in a BPA building that was surrounded by a fence, and was always locked. While Julie hated working on shifts, she was happy that she was still able to enjoy her relationship with Mike.

Julie's hard work and tenacity earned her yet another promotion. The couple was over the moon when they heard the news. Julie's new title was "pool operator." When Mike heard what her role in the company would be, he became a little worried time and time again. Part of the pool operator's job was making rounds to all the substations to check on them and record any issues that needed fixing. This work was mostly scheduled during the day, but sometimes Julie had to go at night also. This concerned Mike, "If she worked nights, I'd follow her in my truck, but I really never worried about her on the job during the day, and neither did she. I did worry about her sometimes at night." The substations were in isolated areas, and having his wife drive alone all the way was something Mike was never comfortable with. However, the position brought in more money for the couple, and they started making bigger plans for their futures.

As Julie's career quickly took off, Mike began enjoying his own successes. His commercial painting began attracting more clients in Spokane than he had ever had in Seattle. Soon enough, he was getting more work than he could ever hope to handle by himself. He started looking for help with the business. The couple soon made enough to buy their own property, and they settled for a 14-acre property about twenty miles away from Spokane. The property was just outside the little town of Deer Park. It featured a nice little house, complete with a barn. This was the best part of the property for Julie, who was finally in a place where she could get and tend to her own horses. Mike, ever the wonderful husband, was finally able to fulfill Julie's wish of getting a horse. The couple bought two horses, Sonn and Tony. Sonn, a palomino quarter horse, was Tony's mother. Tony was a chestnut brown. In addition to the horses, the couple also had two cats, Shakes and Si. Shakes was a black and white cat, while Si was a Siamese cat.

The new house was a source of joy for both of them, but particularly for Julie. She promptly began decorating the home, buying gingham curtains, and even matched the pillows by using the same fabric. The pillows featured a variety of color schemes including blue, pink, white, and mint green. She got interesting decorative items, including a hand-carved "Home Sweet Home" plaque. She covered the sunken living room floor with a delft-blue carpet, and placed a braided rug in front of it. The couple was looking forward to breaking out their fireplace in the winter. The new house, the pets, and the horses were just the beginning of a future they were looking forward to.

Once they had settled into their home, Julie and Mike began planning the next step: babies. Although Julie was not yet pregnant, they had decided that one of them would have to leave work and become a stay-at-home parent. It wasn't automatically decided that Julie would be the one to stay home. Both were okay with whoever got to do it. The peace and quiet existence of their relationship continued, with their professional lives and personal lives going superbly well.

As Mike put it, "Things were just starting to come together."

Disappearance

In September of 1987, Julie and Mike were busy planning out how they would get through the winter months. They needed to get in hay for the horses, and the chilly weather was bound to make Julie's work even more challenging. The winter storms were known to cause increased power outages as lines snapped under the increased weight of the snow. Julie knew that this meant she would soon be having the busiest time during the winter months. On the other hand, winter meant that Mike would have less outdoor work, and would only be getting indoor jobs. The couple wasn't worried, as they had gotten used to sharing the financial responsibilities over the years. Julie admittedly earned more than Mike, and was more than willing to take on a bigger financial role when the circumstances dictated.

On September 15, 1987, Mike and another painter headed out for a job in Ritzville, a small town located eighty miles from his home in Deer Park. Mike expected to be gone until the next day, Wednesday the 16th. As was customary, Mike made a point to call Julie after she left work. That Tuesday evening, the two talked about Mike's business. "Things were normal. She told me she had been to our accountant and everything looked fine. She did the books for my business. I told her I would try to be home late the next night, but I'd call her at five to let her know for sure," Mike told Rule. Knowing that Julie might head to tend to the horses after work the next day, he asked her to remember to carry the cordless phone with her. She agreed, and Mike promised to call the next day. After talking to Julie, Mike and his colleague went back to painting, but did not make enough progress to allow them to head home on Wednesday as Mike had hoped they would. That Wednesday evening, Mike called Julie at around 5 p.m. to let her know that he would be spending the night in Ritzville again. The phone rang and rang, and Julie never picked up. The painting job was far from complete, so Mike headed back to the house and carried on. He planned to go back to the phone booth to call Julie again in a few hours.

"I tried calling Julie again at 7:30 and there was still no answer. Tried again at eight. Same thing. I kept getting my own voice on the recorder. I wasn't worried because I knew that Julie was probably over at our horse trainer's house. Sally only lives eight miles from us, and when I'm gone, they visit a lot," he said. Believing that his wife was safe at home, Mike went back to painting, and took a break when he went to pick the pizza he had ordered. They ate quickly then went back to painting. The made tremendous progress that night, and the two finally called it a night at around midnight. They made a plan to complete the remaining part of the work early in the morning, and then head home. The two headed to the motel ready to sleep off the day's exhaustion. This was not to be.

When Mike got to the motel, he found a note hanging on his room's door. It read, "Call BPA. Your wife's been kidnapped." It took a moment for Mike to register what the note meant. He then took off running, headed to the nearest pay phone. When he got into contact with the power company, he was only provided with minimal information. According to the person on the other end of line, Julie's BPA van was found parked outside the station Julie had last visited, the Spring Hill substation. The station was close to the Riverside State Park. He was told that the van was empty, and that Julie was nowhere to be found. As his mind worked to process the information, he saw a Ritzville police car pull into the motel's parking lot. The officer in the car got out and walked to Mike. He told Mike that he had been looking for him to ensure that he got the message about his wife's disappearance. The officer then told Mike not to rush to Spokane, as they would arrest him if he was caught speeding. Undeterred by the officer's threat, Mike got into his truck and stepped on the gas. Fortunately, he got to Spokane without getting arrested. Mike walked into the Spokane County Sheriff's Office still dressed in his work clothes. His hair and clothes were spattered with paint. In the hour it took to get to Spokane, Mike's thoughts were in high gear. He refused to believe that his wife was missing, and was sure that she would be found by the time he got to Spokane. It was all he could do to keep himself from going crazy.

A sheriff's deputy at the station apprised him of what investigators knew about the disappearance at the time. Julie had been due at the BPA headquarters at around 4:30 p.m. after her visit to the Spring Hill substation. However, police got a call at 9:30 p.m. from a resident in the Spring Hill area. The people residing in the area had noticed the BPA van parked outside the substation with its tailgate window and door open. They had become concerned when it remained there for hours, and they finally decided to reach out to authorities. Officers immediately treated it as a case involving foul play, and the investigation began with earnest. After leaving the sheriff's office, Mike called Don Miller, his closest friend. The two made their way to the scene of Julie's disappearance, and were greeted by a daunting sight.

The area was well lit, with floodlights shining in the area. The road had been closed off, and the two men could see deputies searching the area with flashlights. There were handlers with German Shepherds searching the area, but the dogs kept circling back to the van. As he observed the scene in front of him, Mike was finally able to get more information about what the police had found at the scene. When deputies had gotten to the scene, they immediately noticed the hard hat lying on the ground at the front of the driver's side of the BPA van. Inside the van was Julie's purse and car keys. A closer look at the scene revealed the telltale signs that a struggle had occurred at the scene. Julie was five feet four inches tall, and only weight about 110 pounds. The scene showed that despite her slight frame, she had put up a great fight with whoever had attacked her. The ground and rocks from the driver's side to the front of the van was greatly disturbed. The van itself, which had been covered in a layer of dust, had what seemed like sliding marks created by jeans. Julie always wore jeans, a hard hat, and heavy boots to work. The theory that Julie had been abducted became even more apparent when deputies noticed the deep tire marks in the gravel that seemed to indicate another car had peeled off from the scene. Mike was devastated. This information seemed to make it more certain that Julie might not be coming home, but he was not ready to accept that. He stated, "I expected to find Julie that first day. I thought, 'Well, somebody took her and they probably raped her. But she's out there, and she'll be okay, and we can handle it together.'"

Search and Investigation

Despite the sheriff's office quick mobilization of deputies to start the search for Julie, it soon became clear that it was going to be an uphill task. Mike was immediately considered a suspect, something he had already anticipated. He fully cooperated with the detectives, providing them with any information they needed. He wanted the police to clear him as soon as possible so that they could focus their attention on the case. When he was asked to take a polygraph test, he readily agreed. Just as he had expected, he was soon cleared as a suspect in Julie's disappearance. Investigators soon found themselves without a suspect, and there were no leads generated by the investigation. Julie was well liked at work, and the investigators could not find a single person who wished Julie any harm. Investigators started looking into the whereabouts of men who had a violent history or were arrested for sexual crimes. They found several of them, and one by one they were all cleared. Investigators believed that the most plausible explanation was that Julie had a stalker who followed her to the substation, or who saw her alone at the substation. No leads were ever generated to corroborate this.

At the scene, the sheriff's office had mobilized a great deal of officers to help search for Julie. After an intensive 48-hour search, the efforts proved futile. Mike refused to share the pessimism that the officers seemed to have about Julie's disappearance. He found himself unable to go back to the home he shared with Julie, and instead focused his attention on doing everything he could to find her. With the help of his friends, he started canvassing the area around the Red Hill substation. He knocked on doors and asked the residents questions about that day. He continued this, expanding the area as he went along. When no new information was received, he shifted his focus to searching for Julie in the area. The area was rocky, rugged, and filled with deep crevices. There were lakes and rivers, and Mike knew that the helicopter search of the area had yielded no results. He started mobilizing people to help in the search for Julie. Every weekday morning, there were people who showed up for the search. On weekends, the number rose to hundreds of people. After the sheriff's office stopped the full-time search, Mike rallied friends and neighbors in the search. Some of Julie's colleagues took two weeks' leave to help in the search.

Mike's friends tried to protect him from the media, but as time went on, Mike realized that he needed wider coverage about his wife's disappearance. He began accepting interviews, pleading for anyone with information about Julie's whereabouts to come forward. He mobilized volunteers to distribute thousands of flyers and tens of thousands of buttons with Julie's face. Mike went above and beyond in his search for Julie. This, however, did not please some of the investigators. They felt that Mike's efforts were undermining their investigation. Mike understood the sentiment, "I realized that the police were looking for an arrest and a conviction, and then finding my wife. I wanted my wife back, period. They were worried about my screwing up evidence. Sometimes, I felt I was working against both the police and the person who took my wife." One detective, Mark Henderson, was more accommodating of Mike's efforts. Henderson had met Mike on the golf course a couple of times, and was more forthcoming with Mike about the investigation's progress. Henderson regarded Mike as an ally, and was always ready to hear him out. Mike continued organizing bigger search parties, each involving even more people than the last.

Two months after Julie disappeared, Mike finally went back to their home in Deer Park. The loss he felt was tremendous – and it took years for him to manage to live with the pain. When Ann Rule asked him whether Julie may have left him on purpose, he replied; "No. Never. Of all the scenarios I ever pictured, that would be the easiest for me to accept. But no – not if you knew Julie. She wouldn't leave her horses, and she loves me a little more than she loves her horses."

There have been no sightings of Julie since her disappearance, and her case remains open to this day.

KILLER TEEN : THE TRUE STORY OF KRISTINA FETTERS

JANET NIXON

Kristina Fetters was the youngest woman in the state of Iowa to get sentenced to life in prison without parole after she murdered her great-aunt. But eighteen years later she would be re-sentenced after the Supreme Court ruled that mandatory life sentences for minors was unconstitutional.

Kristina would later be released to a hospice center as she developed breast cancer in prison.

But what happened that fateful night of October 25th, 1994? Kristina was only fourteen years old, five-feet tall and barely one hundred pounds. Yet she committed one of the most brutal assaults in the history of her Iowa town.

This is what transpired in her life before and after she committed a brutal murder of her loving aunt.

EARLY LIFE

She was born Kristina Joy Fetters on February 5th, 1980. The product of a biracial union between her mother Darlene and an African-American man, Kristina did not get to know her father growing up.

Instead, she spent her childhood with Arlene and Wayne Klehm. They were the great-aunt and great-uncle of Kristina but she thought of them as her grandparents. She would refer to Wayne as "Uncle Sheenie" and to her aunt Arlene as "Pooper."

Kristina would play at their home as a young child, swinging from bedsheets tied to a tree in the front yard of the couple's one story home.

Wayne was the easy going one of the couple. Arlene, on the other hand, was the one who enforced discipline on the precocious Kristina.

But Kristina was close to her aunt as were all of her other cousins. Arlene was described as a 'spitfire', a woman who spoke her mind.

"Arlene was just a tiny framed, little woman that would tell you exactly where to go and how you could get there," Kristina's cousin Shanna Sickles said.

Kristina would not meet her biological father until she turned eight years old. She wanted a close relationship with him but the bond never materialized.

"I want him in my life," Kristina said to the Iowa Register in 1996. "I need him in my life. I don't think he knows what he wants."

RUNNING WITH A BAD CROWD

Kristina seemed to have little guidance in her early life. At only twelve-years old, she would meet a twenty-three year old African-American man from Milwaukee named Anthony Leon Hoover. He was a gangster "wannabe", seeking membership into a street gang called the "Black Gangster Disciples." Immature and naïve to the perils of the street, Kristina told the man that she was seventeen years old and ran away with him.

But in June of 1993, Hoover would be arrested on kidnapping charges. He held Kristina at gunpoint, broke her nose and then raped her.

Kristina could not cope with the trauma inflicted by the older man. She would not go to school and would runaway on a weekly basis.

By January of 1994, she was so troubled that she was sent to the Orchard Place, an unlocked facility for minors with behavioral problems. Kristin was placed on Prozac and underwent treatment.

"She was on three different medications that are well known to not play well together now," her friend Jaimi Ross said. "She was showing every warning sign, every red flag that you possibly could on these drugs and they were all ignored."

She also sought solace in Christianity to no avail. A Polk County Juvenile Court officer said that Kristina "lived in a fantasy world most of the time."

Her mother, Denise, would support this assessment as she described her daughter as having hallucinatory episodes.

"She'd say 'look, look, there's Johnny. He's laying on the floor," Denise said. "There's a knife in his head. He's bleeding. Somebody help him, somebody help him. And the teachers would try and re-direct her, you know, you need to get up here and finish your homework."

In September of 1994, her Uncle Wayne would die, Aunt Arlene then sent her grand-niece a handwritten letter, trying to smooth things over.

"Let's be nice to each other and forgive me if I hurt you," Arlene Klehm stated in the letter.

But Kristina would not take the olive branch of her great-aunt.

PLOTTING A MURDER

Ten months later, on October 25th, 1994, Kristina and her roommate Jeanie Fox escaped from the Orchard Place.

Their destination was Kristina's great-aunt's home in Polk County, Iowa.

Arlene Klehm was 76-years old and had little contact with her grand-niece since her placement into the mental health facility.

Living in her fantasy world, Kristina concocted the idea that her aunt Arlene had a lot of money. She planned to escape from the facility, kill her aunt and ride off into the sunset in her truck. What her plans were beyond that, she didn't know.

All she knew was that she needed a partner in crime.

First, she approached a girl named Jessica Wilhite. She explained that her aunt had a lot of money and it would be an easy kill. They could take both her money and her truck after doing the deed.

Jessica remained non-committal.

Kristina then went to Tisha Versendaal and told her of her plan.

"She sits in a chair all day," Kristina said. "I'll stab her then cut her throat. She keeps her money in a safe. We'll take all her money then get away in her truck."

But she found no taker in Tish who was due to leave the facility soon. Instead, she settled on Jeanie Fox, who wanted out of the facility.

Telling Jeanie her plan of escaping and leaving the part of killing her aunt out of the equation, the two packed their bags. They left the facility without incident and that is when Kristina told Jeanie of her other plans.

"Do you want to come with me to kill my aunt?" Kristina asked.

A FIELD TRIP TO MURDER

The girls stopped at three different homes before heading off to kill her aunt. The final stop was at the apartment of a friend where Kristina got a small paring knife.

"What do you need that for?" the friend asked.

"I'm going to kill my aunt," Kristina laughed as she left the apartment.

The two girls arrived at Klehm's home and noticed that a van was parked outside.

Her aunt was entertaining company.

Kristina wanted to wait as she didn't want any witnesses.

The two girls then knelt behind a fence and waited for her aunt's friends to leave.

"I am going to fucking kill her," Kristina repeated the sentence like a mantra outside the home. "Satan has given me the power to do so."

Her aunt's visitors finally left and the two impatient girls knocked on the door. The old woman let them both in, unsuspecting of what the girls had in store for her.

The three small-talked in the kitchen before Kristina pulled Jeanie into a side room.

"I'm going to fucking kill her," Kristina said, again like a mantra as if she were psyching herself up.

Gathering up the nerve, Kristina marched into the kitchen where her aunt was sitting and smashed her over the head with a tea kettle.

Arlene fell to the ground. She tried to get up, woozy, and asked what happened.

Kristina showed no mercy. She exchanged the kettle for a heavy metal skillet and smashed it across her aunt's head.

"Give me the knife," Kristina called out to Jeanie.

Taking the paring knife, Kristina tried to slice Arlene's throat but the knife wasn't sharp enough. She then rummaged through the kitchen drawers, found a larger knife and stabbed her aunt in the back.

"Anthony!" Kristina cried out with every stab (according to Jeanie). "Anthony! Anthony!"

"Help!" Arlene wailed at Jeanie who stood and watched. The bloodied woman wobbled over to the phone but Kristina got there first.

"No!" the teen girl said, ripping the phone off the hook.

Kristina would stab her aunt a total of five times in the back. There were also defensive wounds on her hand and lumps on her head.

Her aunt now dead, Kristina wanted a change of clothes. But first she rummaged through Arlene's bedroom, stealing her necklaces and other small pieces of jewelry.

"We need to find her damn keys," Kristina called out to Jeanie.

They searched for the keys to both the safe and the truck to no avail.

Kristina then thought she heard police sirens in the distance. The two girls began to run and Kristina started to cry.

The girls ran down the block, pounding on the doors of neighbors until police arrived.

"I killed my aunt," Kristina sobbed. "I killed my aunt."

"It was a grisly scene," Detective Neil Schwartz recalled as he came upon Arlene's body. "Brutal. Very bloody."

THE AFTERMATH

Kristina would be charged with first-degree murder and her case was transferred from the juvenile system to a district court in order for her to be tried as an adult.

Her defense team would enter a plea of insanity. She would undergo psychiatric examination with Dr. Michael Taylor who stated that he didn't think Kristina was insane but rather had a personality disorder.

Her planning was too precise and her deception upon entering her aunt's house did not suggest that she was insane, the doctor explained. Furthermore, she understood what she had done after the killing.

But another psychiatrist, Dr. Gaylord Nordine, believed that Kristina was in a psychotic state caused by the Prozac. Dr. Taylor disagreed, stating that Prozac would not have had any adverse consequences on her and that Kristina was also on Thorazine at the time which should have made more her even more docile.

"In talking with her I found absolutely no evidence of any type of psychiatric disorder, " Taylor said. "And in talking with her I found absolutely no indication that she was doing anything on October 25, 1994, other than killing her aunt."

On December 18th, 1995, Kristina would be sentenced to life in prison without parole.

She would serve out her sentence at the Iowa Correctional Institution for Women in Mitchellville, Iowa. She would file appeal after appeal as her attorneys would bring up the fact that this was cruel and unusual punishment for a juvenile.

According to her friends, Kristina didn't forgive herself for what she had done.

"When everybody else was telling her that they forgave her and they're showing her unconditional love," Jaimi Ross said. "She didn't feel she deserved it. It was very hard for her to accept."

Kristina and Jaimi would becoming close friends in jail. They had to...They were two children in an adult prison who were serving life sentences.

When other children came into the facility, Kristina and Jaimi would serve as mentors of sorts.

"They came in and everybody would share their story. It would be Kristina, myself, and another inmate. We'd just open ourselves up and let it all pour out and let them see us for the same flawed humans that they are."

A TERMINAL ILLNESS

In 2013, however, Kristina would be diagnosed with inoperable breast cancer. By November of that year, Kristina would be re-sentenced to life in prison with the possibility of parole.

The judge also recommended that she be immediately paroled due to her illness.

The decision on whether or not to set her free set off a firestorm of controversy in Kristina's own family and the state of Iowa.

"To give her her last few moments of joy and peace," Kristina's mother Denise Fetters said. "I think could be the best thing that she could receive."

But other family members weren't so keen on that idea.

"I just don't feel bad for Krissy for where she's at," Kristina's cousin, Shanna Sickles said. "She put herself there. She didn't give my Aunt Arlene the opportunity to die with her loved ones. Bottom line, if you get life in prison without the possibility of parole, it's life."

But Kristina also had her supporters in friend Jaimi Ross.

"I completely understand when people say things like 'Oh, a life for a life, she took a life, she should die in prison,'" Ross said. "That states more about where you're at in life, and not her, not me and not her family. I get that that's where your heart is and that's what you believe. Were not asking for her to have a second chance."

The parole board decided to release Kristina on a hospice-only basis. There was outcry from people who wanted her to stay in jail, stating that the prison only set her free to save on medical costs.

In the end, the bureaucracy mattered little as Kristina had already reached stage four with her cancer.

"No one can alter the past," Kristina's aunt Darcy Olson said. "It is what it is, this happened to our family and it's now time for my family to have closure. Kristina's impending death cannot be denied and while there have been negative comments, we believe, as the victims, our family has suffered enough and we ask the parole board to grant our request."

Darcy was the only family member aside from Kristina's mother that supported her during the trial and parole hearings.

"It's just so bitter sweet," Olson said. "This has been a 19-year old tragedy for my family. This will bring closure for my whole family and help us all cope just a little bit better with the situation."

"Everybody's like, well, she was a monster," Ross said. "She was evil. It would be so easy in this world if that were just the case. But that's not the way that it is. Not everybody that commits a crime...not everybody that's a sinner is evil or a monster. Her legacy, I hope, will challenge other people to see what they can do for kids. For teenagers. Before it gets to the point where they're in prison or needing to go before a judge for any reason."

The cancer would spread throughout her bones and spine. Kristina would live out her last days in pain.

"The screams I had to listen to last Sunday, no mother should ever have to hear in her life," Kristina's mother, Denise said.

Seven months into her release, Kristina would die at the age of thirty-four.

BRITTANY HOLBERG

JOHN HOLSTON

Brittany Holberg was a twenty-three years old prostitute when she was convicted of murdering 80-year-old A.B. Towery Jr, stabbing him over sixty times.

The controversy surrounding the case centered around the relationship of Brittany and Towery prior to the killing. Brittany argued that Towery was a client who went into a rage when he found drugs on her person. He attacked her and she retaliated in self-defense.

Further investigation would reveal otherwise, however, as Brittany would use numerous household items in a brutal assault on the elderly man.

She fled the scene only to be caught at a McDonald's after police received a tip from a witness who saw her on "America's Most Wanted."

With her good looks and well-proportioned body, Brittany has remained in the spotlight as she was featured in a Maxim Magazine article as one of the "hottest women on death row".

Brittany still sits on death row today with her case being appealed on the numerous levels in the court system.

EARLY LIFE

Brittany was born on January 1, 1973, in Amarillo, Texas.

Accounts on Brittany's home life vary as she would manipulate according to the needs of her listener. To her probation officer, she informed them that her home life was "good" and that she "had everything that she ever wanted". She would often describe her mother as her best friend.

During other occasions, however, Brittany would paint a different story.

She would describe her parents as being "hippie-drugsters". Brittany would state that she was close to her mother but never knew her father, a heroin addict who was in and out of the Texas prison system. Her mother would later marry a man named John Schwartz with the couple marrying and divorcing four times.

They would drink heavily and openly smoke weed in front of the young Brittany who would be sexually assaulted by a babysitter at the age of five. When she was twelve, one of her aunts was murdered and according to Brittany "everything fell apart" at home. Her parents would leave her unattended as they indulged in pot and booze.

"They just stopped working," Brittany said. "They just let everything go."

She would be gang raped by two men who confronted her in an alley behind her home when she was thirteen.

Brittany would then spend the majority of her time living with her grandmother. By the age of sixteen, however, she would run away with her boyfriend Ward. The two would make it as far as California, get married, and have a young daughter named Mackenzie.

The union would not last long, however. Brittany would divorce Ward and move back to her native Amarillo. Ward would take Mackenzie and move to Tulsa, Oklahoma.

Brittany would state that she suffered a knee injury and would become addicted to pain medication during treatment. She would then graduate to harder drugs like cocaine.

In and out of rehab, Brittany's life spiraled out of control. She could manipulate with the best of them, however, and would escape from the Midland Halfway House with the help of a female counselor.

Brittany would hang out with the drug-using crowd and her own habits were out of control. To support her addiction, Brittany began working as a prostitute.

This would put her in harm's way on many an occasion as she would get gang-raped and beaten severely.

The assault would put her in the hospital but she would resume "tricking" when she was released.

"At that point in her life, Brittany was incorrigible," forensic psychologist Paula Orange said."Numerous people had reached to her and tried to help. She had extended family members trying to help.

Friends trying to help. Even church outreach workers. All to no avail. The drugs had taken root and she was dead set on manipulating everyone around her. Family, roommates, church members, doctors, dentists, and pharmacists would all fall victim to her schemes to get drugs."

By 1993, Brittany was a full-blown drug-addicted prostitute with the rap sheet to prove it. In April of that year, she would steal a gun from her step-father. She then passed over $1300 in "hot" checks and applied for several store credit cards using a fake name.

Brittany and one of her aunts would run a scam on dentists, lying to them about their pain levels in order to get prescription medication. When the prescription drugs ran out, she would return to street drugs like cocaine and heroin. Arrests would follow and Brittany would be charged in Hale County with drug possession, paraphernalia, and public intoxication.

Upon her release, Brittany would proceed to steal her mother's car and forge checks in her name. The prostitution continued unabated as well as she stole the wallet from one of her "tricks" who pressed charges.

While in jail for the theft, Brittany would be introduced to Ella Gibbs and Patricia Karnes who ran the ministry in the Randall County Jail. The women tried to get Brittany on the right track and introduce her to Christianity.

"I wanted to reassure Brittany that she is a valuable person, that her life has great potential, and that this is the mortal portion of an eternal life," Karnes said. " Brittany is an eternal being and through the many prayers from my [prayer] group [in Lubbock,] I have been led to come back into this child's life to support her here, to encourage her, to find her courage from the Holy Spirit within her, and to let her know that there is a human being mortal person who will stand beside her and see the good in her and support whatever God plans for the rest of your [sic] life."

A.B. TOWERY

Towery was by all accounts a nice man. His son would bristle at the idea that he was Brittany's "sugar daddy".

"Dad wasn't a dirty old man," his son said. "Dad was just trying to help somebody and look what he got, and now she's getting three meals a day and a warm place to sleep."

The defense would later bring up the fact that he once pulled a knife on his son Russell during a temper tantrum. Towery would have a history with prostitutes (according to court testimony). Connie Baker would be a prostitute from the 1980s to 1997 and stated that Towery was one of her clients. Baker would also claim Tower as a client but she also had a history of drug possession and auto theft. Diana Wheeler would also admit to being one of Towery's prostitutes in the years of 1994 and 1995. She had come to his home and he even went so far as to clean the stains off his Mel Mac dinnerware. But Wheeler also had a long criminal history like Baker, arrested for prostitution, criminal trespass and giving false identification to a police officer.

The controversy at the trial was if Brittany and Towery had an ongoing "sex-for-money" relationship.

This would be vigorously discounted by family members.

His daughter-in-law would come to the home and help with some housekeeping. His sons would also visit daily and never report any "ladies of the evening" coming to visit their father.

The picture just didn't fit.

Brittany stated she was sent to Towery's place by a fellow streetwalker who went by the moniker of "Green Eyes" but that it was later revealed that no such prostitute by that name existed. Brittany had lied like she had so many times before.

The two seemed to have met by chance.

COMING BACK FROM THE GROCERY STORE

November 13th, 1996 was another normal day for the 80-year old A.B Towery. He had just purchased groceries at an Albertson's store and was walking back to his apartment. As he entered the courtyard, he was approached by the 23-year old Brittany Holberg.

She asked to use his telephone and Towery consented. He wanted to help the sweet-voiced Brittany and didn't believe that she posed any kind of physical threat to him.

What he didn't know was that Brittany was coming down from a cocaine high and had not slept in ten days.

"Brittany could be persuasive," Orange said. "She was well-versed in how to charm people, she knew exactly what to say and do in terms of body language. She was like a trained actress. It didn't take much cajoling on her part to convince Towery to let her inside his home. He probably thought 'what's the big deal?'"

Once inside, Brittany would demand money from the elderly man but he refused. Brittany then attacked Towery, trying to strong arm the wallet out of his pocket. The struggle began in the living room. The two then pushed and pulled each other around a partition that separated the kitchen from the living room. They then returned to the living room. At some point, Towery tried to leave the apartment but Brittany pulled him back in. The evidence also indicated that the two paused during this 45-minute fight, catching their breath and nursing their wounds. Brittany would sustain minor stab wounds to her stomach and thigh.

"This was most likely a fight that had a lot of clutching and grabbing," Orange said. "There was less blood in the living room so the conjecture is that is where the fight started. There was blood near the door so that suggests that Towery was bleeding out and trying to escape for help. Remember, he was a slow-moving 80-year old man. Brittany was a young woman but she was fueled by cocaine. He's getting tired a lot faster than she will."

Eventually, Brittany gained the upper hand. She used various objects around the home to beat down Towery. She started with a cast iron frying pan, then a steam iron, a claw hammer, a fruit knife, a butcher knife and then two forks. Towery would fall to the floor, a bloody mess.

Brittany then took a lamp and shoved its base five inches down his throat which choked him to death.

Satisfied that he had finally killed Tower, Brittany removed her bloody clothes. She washed up in his bathroom then went to his closet to find some clothes that fit her.

Walking back to his dead body, Brittany retrieved the wallet out of Towery's pocket. She took out the $1400 dollars he had and dropped the now empty wallet onto his stomach.

Brittany casually walked out of the apartment and hitched a ride with a young couple. The couple dropped her off at a local crack house where Brittany paid them off with two $100 bills (which had blood stains on them). Inside the drug den, Brittany befriended the proprietor and changed clothes again. She then went to a local hotel with hundreds of dollars worth of cocaine and indulged.

TRIAL

Brittany's defense attorney, Catherine Brown Dodson, would argue that Holberg acted in self-defense when she killed Towery. Her primary argument was that Towery was far from an innocent, elderly man. He was, in fact, a drug abuser himself who became physically violent with Brittany when he found a crack pipe on her person. He then hit Brittany two times in the head when she turned her back to him. Brittany retaliated and ultimately put the lamp post in his mouth in an attempt to end the fight.

Brittany then fled as she believed that no one would believe her side of the story because she was both a prostitute and a drug addict.

While in jail, Brittany would try to coerce Katina Dixon, her cellmate to kill Vickie Marie Kirkpatrick who was the prosecution witness.

Towery's history with prostitutes would be brought up in court testimony. They would also mention incidents of violence with his ex-wife and children but jurors didn't believe the old man was in any type of shape to employ the service of a prostitute.

"My father didn't even like the word 'sex'", one of his sons said. "He was old-fashioned."

A psychiatrist would testify, however, that Brittany had battered wife syndrome, post-traumatic stress disorder, and cocaine addiction.

The jury did not take long to deliberate, finding Brittany to be a cunning, manipulative liar who committed one of the most brutal crimes in the history of Amarillo.

They would find her guilty and Brittany would be moved to death row at Gatesville, Texas.

"I can't even explain to you," Brittany said in a magazine interview. "What it's like to have someone say 'You are sentenced to die.' It's words. You feel helpless, numb. It's almost as if your emotions shut you down."

Brittany would spend her first few weeks in prison laying prone on her bed in a zombie-like state. Over time, she grew accepting of her situation. She knew she was going to die but made it a point to learn to take each day one step at a time.

Her inspiration for cleaning up her act came from the memory of her daughter Mackenzie.

"I cannot live," Brittany said. "And I cannot die, knowing that my child has to live with the horror that these people tried to say about me, the story of the crime, their depiction that I was a cold-blooded person."

Brittany states that she dedicates her days to reading, writing to family and working on her law appeals. She also is anti-death penalty advocate.

She would follow other Texas inmates who were now on death row and make appeals on their behalf, specifically that of Betty Lou Beets.

"I realized," Brittany said. "It doesn't matter whether I'm guilty or innocent, this has now become a very political thing... At this point, they're just killing to kill."

She complained that after a recent jail uprising, the treatment of death row inmates has worsened.

"You would not believe the treatment we are given," Brittany said. "Just two weeks ago, we were informed that not only would we be strip-searched for our one hour of recreation a day, but also when taken for a shower. So for the last two weeks, we have been stripped no less than six times a day. This is every day, sometimes at times like 2:30-3 a.m., and we never leave the building or our cells for that matter."

As of this writing, Brittany's stay of execution has been appealed and appealed for the past eighteen years.

Her attorneys would exhaust the appeal process in the state system but it is now in the federal courts.

Her case, however, has been costing taxpayers "conservatively to be at least $400,000" according to county criminal attorney James Farren. In the future, he has decided to forgo seeking the death penalty in capital cases.

Farren continues to favor a death penalty but only under certain circumstances like "a guy walks into a day care center and kills the children or if someone kills a police officer or a firefighter in the line of duty."

Farren predicted that Brittany would remain on death row for another five years at least. "They can go through the U.S District Court in Amarillo, then it can go to the Fifth U.S Circuit Court and the U.S. Supreme Court. Then from there it can go back to the U.S. District."

But the appeals can come to a halt if the district judge refuses to hear it again.

"If the Supreme Court says 'no,'" Farren said. "That's when the district judge can feel safe in stopping this process."

The entire process has been an infuriating one for the Towery family. His son both rages and mourns about what happened to his father.

"She tried to apologize to us during the trial," Russel Towery said. " I got up and walked out. I'm sure other families are going through the same things I'm going through. It's been almost 19 years ... people forget."

"I don't want to die before she does. I want to stand there as she's kicking and screaming going to the death gurney. I want her to think about what my dad went through when she didn't even know his name," he said. "She thinks that because she said she was sorry, that everything's all right. ... she is evil and needs to be destroyed."

KILLER TEEN NIKKI REYNOLDS

SAMANTHA REED

It is not often that stories appear where we find the perpetrators of violence being children and the victims being parents. Although, scattered throughout history it has been seen that children can be capable of shocking amounts of violence, and many, assuming their innocent nature, fall victim to them. In Coral Springs, Florida in 1997 one such story took place. And still the actions of the evening resonate throughout the community.

In The Beginning

Born in 1979 to a mother that didn't want her, Jacquiline "Nikki" Reynolds was adopted by Robert and Billie Jean Reynolds three months after her birth. The Reynolds were a loving, Christian family from Coral Springs, Florida and they were delighted to welcome their new daughter into their lives.

There was nothing that they wouldn't do for Nikki. Robert Reynolds worked for the Department of Transportation and Billie Jean was an administrative assistant at RJ Reynolds. They had a quiet home and they were devoted to making their daughter happy.

Nikki was a good child. She was devoted to the church, like her parents, and she loved her parents deeply. She would go to the mall with her mother or watch baseball games with her father. She could never spend too much time with them. The Reynolds did everything to ensure that Nikki was being raised in a loving and non-judgmental environment.

Friends and family would agree that the environment was loving, but the Reynolds gave Nikki everything she wanted. She was pampered, she was spoiled, and in the end, she was a bit of a brat. Sometimes the best intentions can have the worst consequences.

Still, Nikki, as she got older, became a good student and didn't act out. She achieved good grades in school and went out of her way to become involved in extra curricular activities. She also stayed heavily involved with the church alongside her parents.

By all appearances, Nikki was the perfect child. She was the child that most parents dream of having and Robert and Billie Jean were delighted with her. But children grow up, despite anything that their parents try to do to stop it, and Nikki was no exception. And not all children grow up in a manner that their parents can be proud of.

The Beginning of the End

Nikki went from being the model child to what most people would call a 'troubled teen'. It didn't start in the way one would expect, with failing grades and a lack of interest in school. It started with a lie, and one that shocked family and friends in the disturbing nature of it.

In 1996, sixteen-year-old Nikki came home from school and claimed that she had been assaulted after getting off of the school bus. Naturally her parents were shocked and appalled to hear that this had happened to her. They immediately called the police to handle the situation officially. Nikki claimed she had been attacked by someone she knew, at first. But when questioned by the police her story quickly changed.

She went on to say that she didn't know her attacker and then that the attack hadn't happened at all. She hadn't been raped. She'd made the whole story up.

Now why would a sixteen-year-old, devote Christian girl make up a story about being raped? Why would she go to the extreme of telling her parents and getting the police involved if it was just a story?

It turns out that Nikki hadn't been raped. Rather she was in a relationship, the first one of a sexual nature in her lifetime, and she was terrified to tell her parents about it. She was worried about what they would think about their daughter sacrificing her morals and her principles just to have a boyfriend. But Carlos Infante was her entire world. The sixteen-year-old classmate was consuming her life focus to the point that she hadn't hesitated to throw caution to the wind.

And when the thought of telling her parents about what was going on had come up, in her mind, fabricating a rape story had seemed like a better idea. Nikki was also concerned that she might be pregnant, a worry that was quickly put to rest, but it also influenced her decision to pursue the rape narrative.

Billie Jean was extremely unhappy with Nikki, potentially for the first time during her parenting of the girl. She didn't like the fact that Nikki had a boyfriend. She didn't like the fact that she'd sacrificed her principles and morals, the beliefs that they thought they'd instilled into her all for some boy. They believed that they'd raised a good, Christian girl and for the first time they were starting to question that belief.

Bille Jean and Robert disliked the idea of Nikki having a boyfriend, it didn't particularly matter who he was. They viewed it as a step down for her. They saw it as a complete abandonment of her belief system, something they had strived to instill in her over the course of her entire life. She was sacrificing everything in order to be with this boy, from their point of view. She was losing herself in him. And Billie Jean and Robert wanted to help get Nikki back on a clear path, on a Christian path.

So, they insisted that she spend less time with Carlos and more time with the church. They hoped that in doing so she would see her wrongdoings and find her true self again. They hoped that in spending more time with the church that she would become closer to the family again and forget about Carlos.

Billie Jean believed that Nikki needed to spend more time with a better group of people, a Christian group of people. She hoped that if Nikki spent time around other good, Christian kids that she would find her way again, that she would find a better crowd. And Billie Jean was willing to go to great lengths to ensure that her daughter found a path that fit with the beliefs and morals of the family.

But sometimes the child, no matter how much they push, cannot realize the hopes and dreams of parents. And sometimes, despite all efforts, things still go wrong.

Rebellion Continues

Teenage rebellion can be a strong force, however, and the more that Billie Jean pushed Nikki to go to church the more she resisted. Nikki said, "I knew that the way I was living was not right in God's eyes, but I did not want to hear all of that." She was too engulfed in her life with Carlos. He was quickly becoming her entire world and nothing else mattered to her. Not her parents, and certainly not her church.

The rebellion was extending into her school life. Nikki, who had once been a good student with marks that her parents could be proud of was now beginning to skip class. Her grades were beginning to fall as a result and she was no longer the academic force that she was before.

It was to the point that Billie Jean and Robert barely recognized the girl that they had raised anymore. Who was this young woman living in their house? She reflected none of the morals and principles they had raised her to uphold. She wouldn't listen to them. She opposed them at every turn. They began to wonder what had happened to their daughter Nikki. Where had she gone?

Nikki went from a happy-go-lucky child that was a pleasure to be around, a child who was soft spoken and loved to go to church to a girl no one could recognize. She wore dark clothes, she changed her music, she changed her bedroom to dark colours – she became the opposite of herself. It was hard to tell if this was simply teenage rebellion or something more going on. Was this all because of Carlos or was there some deeper problem at play?

She slept a lot, more than any teenager should and she isolated herself from her family. Gone were the days of ice cream and base ball games. She no longer went on trips to the mall with her mother. She no longer went to church with her family. She became disinterested in many things that used to hold her attention, things that used to captivate her. Her whole world now revolved around Carlos.

It was her first sexual relationship with anyone in her life and it had reached the point of obsession. She filled her diary with everything to do with Carlos. Her room was plastered with photos of him. Her every waking moment revolved around him. There was an unnatural intensity to her emotions towards him, an unhealthy intensity. And it was quickly becoming evident that this was a problem.

Naturally, Billie Jean and Robert were very concerned about their daughter's current mental state. She was not herself, and the only thing they could blame was Carlos as he was the only changing factor in her life. It seemed that he was a negative influence on Nikki in many ways. He didn't make good grades as a student, and now her grades were plummeting as well.

Billie Jean was also worried that he was coming over every day, potentially when they were at work. They had no way to confirm this, but she didn't like the idea that he was at the house alone with her while they were at work. It didn't sit well with her.

So Billie Jean put her foot down, perhaps for the first time in her experience as a parent. She began to tell Nikki no, especially when it came to Carlos. And Nikki handled it with the maturity level of a toddler as opposed to that of a teenager. Nikki threw awful tantrums. Billie Jean and Nikki would engage in screaming matches in the house that would result in slammed doors. The result was very wearing on Billie Jean. She found herself screaming at Nikki almost all of the time. This was not what she wanted her life as a mother to be. This was not the girl she had raised. She needed to do something about this, but she was at a loss as to what the solution could be.

And despite the screaming matches and the orders to stay away, Nikki still kept seeing Carlos. It seemed that nothing could keep her from Carlos. She would sneak out at night when everyone was asleep to see him and it didn't matter what the consequences were.

Billie Jean's frustration escalated to the point that one day she confided in a friend saying "Don't be surprised if one day you come home and there's police cars and fire trucks up and down the street 'cause one of us, it'll be me or Nikki, but one of us will be gone."

Billie Jean's prediction would prove to hit a little too close to home in the coming days. And the aftermath would shock everyone.

Intervention

It was May 14, 1997 when the school counselor contacted Billie Jean to tell her that there was trouble with Nikki and Carlos. She asked that Billie Jean come in and speak with her in person and that Billie Jean, Robert, and Nikki come in for a full meeting the next day. Upon visiting the high school, the counselor told Billie Jean that Nikki and Carlos had more than just the usual high school relationship issues to deal with.

That day Nikki had told the counselor that she was pregnant with Carlos' baby. This had naturally prompted the counselor to contact Billie Jean immediately about the issue. Billie Jean, having already dealt with Nikki's questionable honesty with the previous rape accusation, was hesitant to believe the pregnancy claim. She was fairly certain that this was another one of Nikki's schemes, but there was a sure way to determine its legitimacy.

So she took Nikki to the drug store to find out what was what.

The results of the pregnancy test were negative. That didn't mean Billie Jean was any less pleased with her daughter. Nikki called Carlos with the news. And despite having a counseling meeting the next day Billie Jean decided to seek guidance from a higher power. She dragged Nikki away from the phone and took Nikki to see the church counselor.

Nikki spoke with her pastor as they waited to see the counselor. He was supportive as he talked to her about her boyfriend problems and offered her guidance. Their conversation with the counselor did not have the same supportive tone. The counselor spent the session telling Nikki that her mother did not deserve the behaviour she was displaying. She raised her voice and yelled at Nikki. This didn't go over very well.

Nikki removed herself from the office and from the church. She wanted nothing more to do with the impromptu counseling session. And as she stood in the parking lot of the church she even debated removing herself from the family by running away. But she didn't run away, however. Instead, she took a higher ground, something that hadn't been seen from her in almost a year. She went back into the counselor's office and apologized to her mother. And she finished the session with the counselor before returning home with her mother.

Billie Jean believed that they had made a step in the right direction. She would be the one to learn how wrong she was about that fact.

Confusion and Confessions

It was barely an hour after their visit to the counselor on May 14, 1997 that the call came in to 911. At 7:07pm Nikki Reynolds' panicked voice came over the phone saying "I stabbed her repeatedly in the back. There's blood all over her and all over the floor and everything."

Police were at her house in minutes and the scene that they witnessed was one that would stay with some of the officers for years after. When police arrived they found Nikki waiting on her doorstep. One of the officers who responded indicated that "She had blood all over, blood on her legs, blood on her face."

Nikki was placed in the back of the police car and left to wait while the police went to investigate. A tape recorder was left on with her in the police car so that anything that was said while she was alone was recorded and on file. It recorded her praying that her mother was still be alive and saying that she had learned her lesson. She was asking God to forgive her and for her mother to please still be alive.

Her mother was brought out of the house on a stretcher by the EMTs and she was still alive at the time that she left the house. However, Billie Jean was pronounced dead at the hospital at 8:10pm after suffering from 13 stab wounds.

Nikki was taken to the police department immediately. Robert came home from work to find the house in a state of chaos, surrounded by police cars and police tape. He hadn't yet been informed of the situation that had come to pass behind the front doors of his home. He broke down at the news that his wife was gone and that his daughter was responsible. The shock of it was something that he couldn't quite comprehend.

The scene inside the house was gruesome and shocking to police investigators. It depicted Billie Jean's terrible, drawn out death as she fought to get away from her daughter. But there was no escape for her as she was stabbed repeatedly until she finally lay immobile on the floor.

The police found the kitchen knife that had been used as the murder weapon in the sink and it still had blood on it. They also found evidence that someone, likely Nikki, had attempted to clean up the scene using towels and dishcloths. The blood soaked pieces of cloth were scattered about the kitchen unable to handle the sheer amount of blood that had resulted from the incident.

While the police officers worked diligently at the crime seen the detectives questioned Nikki about the murder. And it didn't take too much effort to get her to talk.

"I didn't have any intentions of lying." Nikki said. "I didn't have any secrets. I wanted to get it out." She felt almost compelled to tell the story of what had happened. She needed to let them know.

"It was simple, all I had to ask her was what happened today and just started chatting. She went through the whole story from a to b," said the detective who interviewed Nikki.

The story that was told by Nikki revolved heavily around Carlos Infante, the infamous boyfriend. Nikki had used her fake pregnancy to keep Carlos in a relationship with her when he wanted to leave, fearing what would happen if he left. When she had found out she was not pregnant, for sure, she called him to give the news. Carlos indicated that he wanted nothing to do with her and all of her lies. He'd had enough. Billie Jean had even got on the phone with Carlos and apologized for all of the drama that he'd had to endure at the hands of her daughter.

Nikki had decided then and there that someone would die that day. She even took a handful of aspirin before going to the counseling meeting with her mother at the church. She was certain that she could overdose on it. She was certain that it would be her that would die.

However, when the overdose failed her thoughts went from suicide to homicide rather quickly. But the intended victim had not been her mother.

Her plan had been to get a hold of Carlos the next day and kill him. She figured she could catch him after first hour and slash his throat if she snuck up behind him. She believed that if she couldn't have him then no one should be allowed to have him. He belonged to her essentially.

However, the one obstacle in her plan to kill Carlos was the meeting they had with the guidance counselor the next day. Nikki was unsure whether she would be sent home after the meeting or not. In order to kill Carlos she would have to skip the guidance meeting. So, in order to accomplish this, she figured she would have to kill her parents as well. She would just wait until they were sleeping and then simply slash their throats. Then they could no longer stand in her way.

A real obstacle came into this metaphorical plan when her father left for church after dinner that night alone and her mother stayed home. This was very out of character for them. Nikki also stayed home as her mother told her she was grounded for the rest of the evening. She was instructed to clean the dishes after dinner.

Nikki decided that she would just roll with this change. She believed, since she was now home alone with her mother, that it would be much easier to kill her mother now, clean up the mess, and then wait until her father returned. She could then kill him and do the same. Finally, she could drive herself to school in the morning, wait for

Carlos, and kill him after first hour just like she had planned. It would work out perfectly.

Logical thought was gone at this point in time. Nikki was acting strictly on whatever thoughts came to her mind and they were frantic, desperate. Still, she waited for her opportunity to arrive. She waited for her moment when she could kill her mother.

Opportunity came while she was cleaning up in the kitchen and Billie Jean was working at her computer. Nikki took a kitchen knife, paused for a moment to check the blade for its sharpness, and then slowly approached her mother. She hesitated now that she had the knife in hand. She wasn't sure what it would feel like to slash someone's throat.

When she finally got up the nerve to come up behind her mother and attempt to cut her throat it didn't slash it, it only cut it. Billie Jean jumped up in surprise and darted towards the laundry room. She screamed, "No, Nikki, no."

"I told her I had to kill her because I can't live without Carlos," Nikki explained to police in her interview.

Nikki kept stabbing her because she wanted to put her out of her misery, she claims. She didn't want her mother to suffering any longer. And in her last moments, Billie Jean still offered her daughter forgiveness for killing her.

Nikki spent one night in the hospital because of her claim of ingesting a large amount of Aspirin. After that she was turned over to the county jail where she was formally booked on a charge of First Degree Murder.

The First Trial

The first trial for Nikki Reynolds lasted from April 14, 1999 – May 3, 1999.

If convicted, Nikki faced life in prison after spending two years in a Juvenile Detention Centre. The prosecution built their case around Nikki's obsession with Carlos Infante, making sure to indicate that he was not at fault in any way and rather he was also one of the three listed on Nikki's kill list.

The defence opted to take an insanity plea route, rather than try to dispute the charge that Nikki had committed the murder – something she had confessed to multiple times. This defence fell flat. The criterion for an insanity plea is very strict. The accused has to suffer from a serious mental illness and the accused has to be unaware that what they are doing is wrong or has consequences.

The psychologist that testified for the prosecution indicated that Nikki was well aware of what she was doing, and rather that she was just a confused girl. The defence tried to argue that Nikki suffered from Borderline Personality disorder. They claimed that individuals suffering from this disorder could idolize the individuals they are with and then suddenly snap, and become violent. Which is very similar to Nikki's reaction after Carlos indicated he wanted nothing to do with her. They also claimed that the Aspirin played a part as Aspirin can cause metabolic imbalances and psychosis upon overdoes.

Regardless of the claims on either side, the jury was hung and the trial ended in a mistrial.

The Second Trial

Second trail for Nikki Reynolds began on Sept 1, 1999.

Similar to the first, the prosecution brought a series of psychologists to the stand to prove that, while not a rational act, Nikki was not insane. The prosecution also claimed that her mother's death was premeditated.

The defence countered that Nikki was mentally ill and called experts to speak to Nikki's sanity. The defence also brought forward Nikki's biological mother to testify. The birth mother had a long history of mental illness and family violence. The defence argued that it was the anxiety over losing Carlos that pushed Nikki over the edge and brought her mental illness to the surface.

After much deliberation, Nikki Reynolds was found guilty of Second Degree Murder at the end of the trial.

At the sentencing hearing on January 7, 2000 Nikki's biological mother made a plea to include treatment as a part of Nikki's sentence. She believed that her daughter needed help, much like she had needed help in her lifetime.

Nikki also addressed the court, pleading with the judge to sentence her to a psychiatric facility instead of prison. She truly believed that there had been something wrong that day, if not insanity, than something else. She believed that she needed help. She bore no ill will towards her family. She hated none of them. She had never hated them and still didn't.

However, the judge believed that the wrongness of what she had done to outweigh all else. He gave her the maximum sentence under Florida law, 34 years in prison. She was resentenced to 21 years and 8 months on April 4, 2001 due to a change in sentencing laws in the state of Florida.

In the end Robert Reynolds remarried in 1998 and has had no contact with his daughter since she was sent to prison on January 2000.

And Nikki was incarcerated at the Gadsden Correctional Facility in Quincy, Florida. She was eligible for parole in 2015 and was released.

BLACK WIDOW JUDY BUENOANO

ERIN CARTER

Judy Buenoano loved men. But she loved killing them more.

In 1971, she murdered her husband James and nine years later she would kill her own son, Michael. In 1983, she would attempt but fail to kill her boyfriend, John Gentry. She is also believed to have been responsible for the death of Bobby Joe Morris (another boyfriend) in 1978. She was never convicted of the Morris crime, however, as by the time the authorities had connected the dots she was sentenced to death for the murder of her first husband.

But the suspicions didn't stop with the Morris death. Buenoano is also suspected of killing a man in 1974 and in 1980, another boyfriend would die under suspicious circumstances.

Buenoano would become the first woman executed in Florida since 1848 and only the third woman executed since capital punishment had been reinstated in 1976.

She would be sent to the electric chair in 1998. Her last words were that she wanted to be remembered as a "good mother."

Instead, she would go down as one of the most sadistic female serial killers in American history.

This is her story.

EARLY LIFE

Judy was born Judias Welty in Quanah, Texas on April 4th, 1943. Her father was a day laborer at a local farm. Judy would talk about her mother being a full-blooded member of the Mesquite Apache tribe but little did she know that a "Mesquite Apache" tribe didn't exist.

Her mother would die of tuberculosis when Judy was only two years old. She and her baby brother Robert would be sent to live with their grandparents while their two older siblings would be put up for adoption.

"When Judy's mother died," forensic psychologist Paula Orange said. "It sent Judy's life into a tailspin. This is one of those 'Butterfly Effect' scenarios. A tragic circumstance that occurred early in a child's life that led to her perpetuating pain on everyone else for the rest of her own adult life."

She would eventually leave her grandparents and join her father in Roswell, New Mexico. He had remarried and Judy would claim that both he and her new stepmother would beat, starve, and burn her with cigarettes.

They made her a "house slave", forcing her to do chores around the house at their bidding. Judy would finally act out at the age of fourteen as she would burn two of her step brothers with hot grease. Not stopping there, she attacked both her father and step-mom with fists flying.

Police would be called and Judy would be jailed for over two months. After she served her jail time, the judge gave Judy a choice, either return home or go to reform school. She opted for the latter and was sent to Foothills High School. She would remain there until 1959 when she would graduate at the age of sixteen.

She held her entire family in contempt, particularly her younger brother Robert.

"I wouldn't spit down his throat if his guts were on fire," Judy once said when asked about her brother.

CHANGING IDENTITY

Judy returned to Roswell but changed her name to "Anna Schultz". She found work as a nurse aide and would give birth to a baby boy out of wedlock, Michael Schultz on March 30, 1961. Judy would remain silent on the identity of the baby's father but people believed that Judy was having an affair with a pilot from the nearby air force base.

In 1963, the twenty-two-year-old Judy would marry James Goodyear. Goodyear was twenty-nine years old and serving as a sergeant in the United States Air Force.

They would have their first child together, James Jr, four years later. James would celebrate the event by legally adopting Michael. Daughter Kimberly would come a year later as the family would move to Orlando, Florida.

Judy would then open her own business, starting the Conway Acres Child Care Center in Orlando. She listed James as the co-owner even though he was during a one-year tour in the Vietnam War. After returning home, he only had three months of downtime before he was admitted to the U.S. Naval Hospital in Orlando, complaining from symptoms staff physicians never quite identified. He would die on September 15, 1971.

Goodyear was only thirty-seven years old at the time of death and authorities believed he died due to natural causes.

"He came home from Vietnam ill and he never got well," Judy said. ``It had nothing to do with me. I was not in Vietnam."

"Crazy that Goodyear was able to survive the horrors of Vietnam but not Judy Buenoano," Orange said. "He had no idea he was married to a sociopath. She had no respect for the fact that he had just put himself on the line for her and the country. All she saw were dollar signs."

Judy poisoned James with arsenic and waited almost a week after his death before cashing in his three life insurance policies. A few months later, an "accidental fire" burned down their Orlando home. Judy would receive another $90,000 in fire insurance.

She lost her husband and her home. But her purse was never fatter.

NO GRIEVING WIDOWS ALLOWED

Judy would waste no time finding another man. Despite having three kids in tow, she would find a new love in Bobby Joe Morris when she moved her family to Pensacola.

It was business as usual for Judy as she had a fat bank account courtesy of James Goodyear and a new beau in Bobby Joe. Eldest son Michael, however, was not doing well in school. He scored on the low end on IQ tests and was a behavioral problem. Judy would get him evaluated at a state hospital in 1974 and then sent Michael out to foster care where he would also receive psychiatric treatment.

Judy's new home would suffer another "accidental fire" and she collected money from the insurance. She then took Michael out of foster care and moved to Trinidad, Colorado with Bobby Joe and the rest of her children. Judy then changed her name from "Anna Schultz" to "Judias Morris".

FOUR YEARS MAX

Judy would date Bobby Joe for four years before deciding it was time to cut him loose.

Bobby Joe would start to suffer from the same mysterious illness as James Goodyear did years earlier as he complained of dizziness and vomiting. He would be admitted to San Rafael Hospital on January 4, 1978, but doctors would not be able to pinpoint what was wrong with him. He would be sent home to Judy's care two weeks later. Two days later, however, he would would pitch face-first into his dinner plate, unconscious. He would be rushed to the hospital, but Judy knew that her "medicine" had taken effect.

Five days later, Bobby Joe Morris would be dead. Doctors would chalk up his death to cardiac arrest and metabolic acidosis.

Judy would wait, just like she did after she killed James, before cashing in on Bobby Joe's life insurance.

Authorities were none the wiser.

But Bobby Joe's family suspected something fishy was going on. Back in 1974, Judy and Bobby Joe had been visiting Brewton, Alabama when a man from Florida was found dead in a motel room in that town. Police would find the man in the room after receiving an anonymous call. He was shot in the chest with a .22-caliber weapon and his throat was cut open.

Judy's connection to the crime? Bobby Joe's mother had overheard Judy telling her son about the murder.

"The sonofabitch shouldn't have come up here in the first place," Judy said. "If he came up here he was gonna die."

Bobby Joe had told his mother about the crime on his deathbed. She thought the confession could be attributed to his delirium, but Bobby Joe told her too many specifics to ignore.

"We should never had done that terrible thing," Bobby Joe mumbled to his mother. "Never should have done that to him."

She tipped off police but they would not be able to find any fingerprints inside the room and no bullet was recovered from the corpse. The case remained unsolved.

WHAT'S ONE MORE SURNAME?

On May 3rd, 1978, Judy would change her name again. This go around, she would change her last name to Buenoano, which in Spanish meant "good year." She stated that she meant it as a tribute to her husband James Goodyear and her Apache mother.

Things continued to go bad with Michael as he dropped out of high school in the tenth grade. With limited employment opportunities, he would join the army in June of 1979 and get assigned to Ft. Benning in Georgia after basic training. When he was on his way to his new post, he visited Judy in Pensacola.

Judy greeted her son with open arms. Then she began poisoning him.

By the time he reached Ft. Benning, he felt sick. Army physicians would find seven times the normal level of arsenic in his body.

They could do little to reverse the damage done. Six weeks after his arrival, the muscles in his arms and legs and deteriorated to the point where he was a paraplegic.

"Michael had no use of his legs," Orange said. "And he could not move his arms past his elbow. Again, Judy was a sociopath. It is unfathomable for a normal human being, a mother, to do this to her own child. Yet she did it to Michael. He was always an inconvenience to her but now that he had military insurance he could become an asset in death."

Judy would give Michael the short shrift while favoring James and Kimberly. Michael and James didn't get along well as clearly their mother favored the latter. Judy would hide Michael when people came over because she was ashamed of him. She would have a neighbor named Constance Lang watch over him when visitors arrived.

"Michael didn't fit the picture Judy wanted to present to the world," Orange said. "She wanted to be looked at like a woman of high status. She drove a Corvette and owned her own business. Michael was a slow-thinking kid. She didn't want anyone to see that."

The army didn't investigate the reasons behind Michael's inordinate levels of arsenic. Instead, they set him up with leg braces and a prosthetic device on one of his arms.

He would be discharged from active duty because of the medical disability.

But his mother saw dollar signs.

The day after his return home, Judy wasted no time. She organized a fishing trip with Michael, James, and daughter Kimberly. They would leave Kimberly ashore at the East River bridge while they went into the water with a two-seat canoe. A small folding lawn chair had been placed in the middle of the canoe for Michael who had was outfitted with a leg brace, a fishing reel, and a ski belt.

James would state that had fished for about two hours when they were reaching shore when a "snake fell into the canoe." He said that everyone panicked as the snake slithered around. The canoe hit a log and capsized.

James would claim to have been knocked out by the impact and would remember nothing until he came to inside an ambulance.

He would tell this version to the court but when he was talking to Army investigators, he made no mention of a snake.

"There is conjecture as to how much James was involved or much did he know," Orange said. "The statement given to the army investigators is different from what he would state later in court. The statement given to the army was a written statement and the handwriting didn't seem to match his own."

A man named Ricky Hicks saw the overturned canoe, an ice chest, and a plastic bag in the river. He also saw Judy and James.

"I lost the other boy," Judy said as Ricky approached them on the shore. "A snake had gotten into the canoe and I tried to hold the snake down with a paddle."

"Where is he?"

"It's no use," Judy said, waving him off.

Hicks said Judy appeared to be concerned about James then asked him for a beer. He then drove Judy's car to a nearby phone and called the county rescue squad.

The rescue team arrived and began looking for the missing Michael.

The canoe had not moved as there was barely a current. They would find Michael's body one-quarter of a mile upriver where the canoe had been rescued. The rescuers stated that it should not have been a problem to swim upstream, suggesting that Michael could have been saved.

Judy initially said that Michael had a life jacket on but later recanted and said that it was a ski belt.

There was no ski belt on Michael when he was found.

Judy would later state that after the canoe capsized, she saw James lying face down in the water. She swam over and cleared his air passage to resuscitate him. She looked around for Michael then was picked up by Ricky Hicks.

"Michael disappeared under water," Judy said. "I went to rescue James. I almost lost both of my sons that day. Mothers just don't murder their children. If I'd have lost both of them, I don't know what I would have done. They would have had to put me in a mental institution."

"Kimberly's boyfriend would later testify that Judy had killed Michael for the insurance money," Orange said. "The children knew about their mother but she had clearly brainwashed them into silence. She provided for them, she fed them. She knew what was best."

Telling the police that she was a "clinical physician", they bought her story of the boat capsizing. The army investigators did not buy her account. Not having any evidence, however, they would eventually pay her Michael's military life insurance ($20,000). Investigators got suspicious, however, when they found out that two civilian life policies were taken out on Michael. The applications on both policies look to have been forged.

Judy's former sister-in-law, Peggy Goeller, would call to inquire how she was doing. She would make no mention of Michael's death during her first call but on a second call she told Peggy that Michael had died "during Army maneuvers".

MOVING ON

Judy would demonstrate very little grief over Michael's death and she would not be charged with his murder. Foremost on her mind was finding another man and another big check.

She opened a beauty salon in Gulf Breeze and found her next mark: businessman John Gentry.

Gentry was more well-heeled than her previous conquests so Judy put on airs for his sake. She told him that she had Ph.D.'s in biochemistry and psychology and was the former head of nursing at West Florida Hospital.

Gentry believed her story and decided to spoil his blue-blooded girlfriend expensive gifts, vacations and the finest cuisine all in the name of courtship.

Pushing the envelope, Judy would encourage John to provide life insurance for both them both. She then secretly boosted Gentry's coverage from $50,000 to $500,000 without him knowing.

Two months later, Judy began giving Gentry "vitamin pills".

"Come on," she said, placing two pills into Gentry's palm.

"What are you, my mother?" Gentry asked.

"Well, God forbid I want to see you healthy," Judy slid the cup of water toward her prey.

Gentry would then complain of dizziness and later begin vomiting after his daily dose of Judy's "vitamins."

He would admit himself into the hospital and noticed that his symptoms disappeared when he stopped taking the vitamins.

Still smitten by Judy, he did not suspect her of wrongdoing. Instead, he took her vitamins and hid them in his briefcase.

One night, however, Judy sat him down for a special dinner. She had a very special announcement.

"I'm pregnant," she said, smiling in triumph.

"Finally," Gentry said. He told Judy that they should celebrate. She told him to go to the liquor store for an expensive bottle of champagne.

"Be right back," he said, kissing her with excitement.

Running out the door, Gentry got into his car and a bomb exploded with he turned the ignition key.

Amazingly, Gentry survived the blast as trauma surgeons saved his life.

"Judy really overplayed her hand with the explosion in the car," Orange said. "Really it speaks to her level of dedication and ingenuity. Who knows where she got the idea, maybe watching the Godfather. But the police found the dynamite residue inside Gentry's car. They decided to look no further than to Judy herself."

Their interrogation and research would unearth lie after lie. They found out about the $450,000 increase in Gentry's life insurance.

Gentry himself thought the insurance had been canceled. He was shocked to learn that she had increased the payout and was paying his premiums out of her own pocket. The police didn't spare him any quarter. They would him that she was not a real doctor and that she couldn't get pregnant.

"What?" Gentry muttered, completely flabbergasted.

Judy had been sterilized seven years earlier.

Gentry couldn't believe his ears. Police would go on to say that she had booked tickets for a world cruise for herself and her children...leaving Gentry out. They discovered that Judy had been telling her friends that Gentry was suffering from a "terminal illness."

The only "terminal illness" Gentry had was Judy Buenoano.

Now fully convinced, Gentry would reach into his briefcase and give police the "vitamin pills" that Judy had been giving him.

"Judy was emptying the vitamin casing and filling it with formaldehyde and a little arsenic," Orange said. "Over time, this would have been lethal."

The state attorney would refuse to charge Judy as they wanted an air tight case in order to prosecute. Knowing that they had their killer, officers, and federal agents searched Judy's home in Gulf Breeze, obtaining wire and tape from her bedroom that looked to match the same wire/tape they found on the bomb in Gentry's car.

They would search her son James' room, finding marijuana and a sawed-off shotgun. He would be jailed him for possession of drugs and an illegal weapon.

"Again, this is a strange mistake on Judy's part," Orange said. "She was meticulous and a good liar. Why she didn't remove any and all evidence from her home is a head-scratcher. She had gotten sloppy because she had gotten away with so many crimes before without so much as a slap on the wrist. She thought she was above the law, got careless and left incriminating evidence behind."

Judy would then be arrested at her beauty salon and charged with attempted murder. It took a month of police work, but authorities would trace the source of the dynamite used in the bomb, linking the Alabama buyer to Judy via phone records which showed numerous long-distance calls from her home.

Judy would pay bail but authorities would not let up. Five months later, she would be indicted for first-degree murder in the death of her son Michael, with an additional count of grand theft for the insurance scam.

Feeling the noose around her neck, Judy would fake a seizure and wind up in Santa Rosa Hospital.

Authorities then exhumed the bodies of the men they believed she killed. Bobby Joe Morris was exhumed with arsenic found in his remains. Identical results were obtained with the exhumation of James Goodyear, in the following month.

Connecting the dots, police obtained a court order to exhume the bodies of all the men that had died while associated with Judy; son Michael, husband James Goodyear, and boyfriend Bobby Joe Morris.

Arsenic would be found in all of the bodies.

"There was enough arsenic in him (Goodyear) to kill twelve people," Detective Ted Chamberlain said. "So he was loaded. I mean that boy was loaded with it when he went down."

OPEN AND SHUT CASE

In 1984, Judy would be convicted of the murders of Michael and attempted murder of Gentry. In a separate trial in 1985, she would be convicted of the murder of James Goodyear in which she would ultimately receive the death sentence.

Judy would be imprisoned in the Florida Department of Corrections Broward Correctional Institution death row for women.

HER FINAL HOURS

Judy would spend her last day watching a hunting and fishing show, eating chocolates, and talking about old times with her children and cousin Jeanne Eaton. She would read a suspense novel called "Remember Me" and her last meal with be steamed broccoli, asparagus, strawberries and hot tea.

Judy's impending execution did not receive the same media attention as Karla Faye Tucker whose was executed only a month earlier. Her execution was opposed by the Pope and Jesse Jackson.

'"She may not have been as photogenic, as young or as pretty as Karla, but she was just as good a Christian," Eaton said.

"Judy obviously had her enablers within her family," Orange said. "How could she be 'just as good a Christian' if she is poisoning people, blowing them up and the 'Christian' she is being compared to is ice-picking people to death. People say the strangest things."

But Judy herself was bitter that no one paid much attention to her presence on death row, particularly the fact that she was a woman.

``Karla was a young female, very attractive and she had become a Christian in prison," Judy said. ``We all prayed that she would be granted a stay of execution and clemency because we felt that she was a different person and she deserved a chance. Possibly, I am a different person. But I was a Christian when I came here. I was a devout Catholic. I've not changed in that."

"It was a bit of a curiosity as to why the media was so charged to prevent the execution of Karla Faye Tucker and paid little heed to Buenoano," Orange said. "Tucker's killings were ferocious and sadistic while Buenoano's killings could be seen as passive. But what drew people to Tucker was her physical appearance and demeanor. She came across as a sweet, reformed choir girl at the end. She had a charming smile and a soft voice. Buenoano, on the other hand, looked sinister. She had squinty eyes, high cheekbones and a snarling, Southern drawl. Her body language and demeanor screamed hostile."

Judy would enter the death chamber with several guards by her side. They strapped her into the large oak chair, placing leather straps over her waist, wrists, chest, and legs.

They fitted the calf and headpiece electrodes last, inserting a wet sponge in between to reduce the burning of Judy's skin.

"Do you have a final statement?" the warden asked.

"No, sir," Judy closed her eyes tight.

The witnesses on the other side of the glass partition watched in silence.

Judy did not look at them as a leather mask was placed over her face.

The warden nodded his head and the switch was pulled.

Steam wafted up from her right leg as her body jolted for thirty-eight seconds. Her hands balled into fists, white knuckling from the shock as smoke rose from her feet to the ceiling.

Then Judy went limp. She would be pronounced dead at 7:08 a.m., March 30th, 1998.

The date was her son Michael's 37th birthday.

BLACK WIDOW KRISTIN ROSSUM

AIMEE BAXTER

Photos of a beautiful, lively little girl, her blonde hair in pigtails as she dances The Nutcracker in her little pink tutu. That same adorable child laughingly enjoying holidays with her family at their home. These are the pictures that Constance Rossum will show you of her daughter Kristin.

Bright, vivacious, and uncommonly beautiful are the words used to describe Kristin Rossum as a child. The child that everyone said was so smart and pretty, the one who modeled for department stores and who excelled in her schoolwork, the one with what seemed to be the perfect suburban childhood.

However, as many already know ... looks can be deceiving.

Idyllic Child becomes a Rebellious Teen

Born to Ralph and Constance Rossum on October 25, 1976, in Claremont, California, Kristin Rossum wanted for nothing. Kristin was the first child of Ralph Rossum – a professor at Claremont McKenna College – and his wife Constance – who worked at Azusa Pacific University. Even when her first and then second little brother was born, Kristin remained her parent's sweet little princess.

When Ralph accepted a position as President of Hampden-Sydney College in southern Virginia, the family moved across the country from California to Virginia. It was 1991 and Kristin was a delicate 15 years old. Her parents enrolled her in an all-girl boarding school in Richmond, Virginia named St. Catherine's School.

That seems to be the beginning of the end of Kristin's innocence. At the private school, Kristin made friends quickly and soon was very popular. She became the party girl smoking, drinking, and using marijuana liberally.

In 1992, at just 16 years old, Kristin is introduced to methamphetamines – a strong Central Nervous System (CNS) stimulant – and is soon hooked. Within a few weeks, she was using Crystal Meth (also known as Crank, Speed, Chalk, etc.) daily. She was a tweaker (slang used to describe a methamphetamine addict).

Kristin the Druggie

When asked about it later, Kristin recalled her first time using meth by saying "I remember it feeling good, a kind of euphoria. You feel very revved up and energetic and happy. I wanted to feel that all the time."

Soon, Kristin's straight As were slipping to become Cs and Ds. She lost weight rapidly and began to withdraw from her family and any friends who were not using meth. According to later court records, Kristin is described as having "an almost insatiable need for crystal meth."

It was not long before Kristin developed all the character traits that addicts hone to conceal and continue their freedom to use. Lying, manipulation, and theft became the new norm for young Kristin Rossum.

Her parents were understandably at a loss for how to deal with this behavior. After all, not that long ago they were tucking her into her pink canopy bed and kissing her goodnight with a song and a prayer. However, the lack of consequences established by her parents could be a contributing factor in her later misdeeds.

At first, they ignored their daughter's erratic and rapidly devolving character, chalking it up to teenage angst. Eventually, they could not turn a blind eye anymore and they soon realized that their daughter was not who they thought she was.

Later, both Ralph and Constance cite an incident in 1993 as the first time they admitted their daughter had a problem. After returning from a cruise in April of that year, the Rossums found that their sweet, perfect daughter had in fact stolen their credit cards, personal checks, and a video camera.

Confronted with the missing items, Kristin pointed to some of her friends (fellow druggies) as the thieves. They say that she admitted to using some of the cash to buy drugs but insisted that the rest was stolen by somebody else. Her parents accepted Kristin's excuse and did not report the theft to police.

According to Constance's testimony later, Kristin's erratic behavior came to a head in December of 1993. Ralph Rossum – convinced Kristin was still using drugs – attempted to search his daughter's backpack. She resisted, they struggled, and he struck her several times in the arm to get the bag away from her.

However, that was not the end of the incident. Sobbing and enraged, Kristin grabbed a knife from the kitchen and slashed at her wrists. When that did not work, she ran upstairs to the bathroom, locked herself inside, and began hacking at her wrists with a razor. Later Kristin told the court, "I felt devastated ... I didn't know how to deal with the situation ... I wanted them to see how sorry I was."

Her wounds, however, were superficial and her parents treated them at home. They later said that they were "afraid of what would happen if they took her to the hospital." They feared that if they told the hospital that she had cut herself, they would have committed her for a psychiatric evaluation and if they tested her blood and found drugs, they would report her to the police.

It is likely that the reason none of the cuts were serious was that Kristin did not intend them to be. Psychologists later speculated that it was merely a way for her to manipulate her parents. If it was, it worked.

Again, Kristin escaped any immediate consequences for her bad behavior. Again, her parents made excuses for her behavior and thus enable her to continue that behavior. Cryptically, one entry in her diary after this incident contained the morbidly, prophetic words, "I could get away with murder."

A few days after this incident, a teacher noticed the marks on Kristin (or she possibly showed them to her intentionally). She called the police to the school to investigate the possibility of child abuse.

Officer Larry Horowitz of the Claremont Police investigated and testified that Kristin told him that her father had hit her and that her mother had "called her a slut and said she was worthless." After interviewing Ralph and Constance Rossum, Officer Horowitz concluded that there had been no abuse and the case was closed.

In January 1994, Constance found a glass pipe hidden in Kristin's underwear drawer. She eventually called Officer Horowitz and Kristin was handcuffed, arrested, and held for several hours at Claremont Municipal Jail.

Kristin finally had her first taste of culpability. She seemed to clean her act up and after graduating, she enrolled part-time at the University of Redlands in California. However, soon she relapsed and dropped out of school without a word to her family and simply disappeared. She moved to Chula Vista – a suburb of San Diego near the Mexican border.

A Chance Encounter

After a month of hard partying, drinking, smoking meth, and hiding from her parents, Kristin was walking the pedestrian bridge that led from Chula Vista to Tijuana, Mexico. Authorities speculate that at the time she was likely on her way to meet her supplier in Mexico on that fateful day.

As she crossed the bridge, Kristin Rossum dropped her jacket. Before she could retrieve it, a handsome young man that she later described as reminding her of John Stamos, had picked it up and was handing it to her. It was Greg de Villers and he later told friends "it was love at first sight." They chatted in French while Greg's younger brother paced nearby.

She returned to the Southern California apartment where de Villers lived with his brothers, Bertrand and Jerome, and a friend, Christopher Wren. She never left.

Within a few weeks, the couple was professing their love and de Villers had sworn to help Kristin kick her meth addiction. Greg's brothers and Wren were not happy and prompted him to end the relationship. They had noticed that things were coming up missing from the apartment since Kristin's arrival and knew of her drug problem.

According to a statement given later by de Villers' friend and roommate Christopher Wren, Kristin had told him that she felt like being with Greg was the wrong choice. For some reason, Wren chose not to tell his buddy.

Even if Wren had told de Villers about Kristin's doubts, it is unlikely that it would have made any difference. Greg de Villers was adamant, he loved Kristin Rossum no matter what her faults and he was going to save her from herself.

By May of 1995, it looked as though he had done just that. By all accounts, it looked like Kristin was clean and free of the hold meth had on her. She reestablished contact with her worried parents and it looked like Kristin was finally moving towards the bright future her parents had envisioned for their little girl.

The Rossums looked at Greg de Villers as if he was an angel for all that he had done for Kristin. Constance Rossum, in an interview with the CBS news magazine "48 Hours," put it like this, "We always called Greg our godsend from heaven. I mean, of all the people she could have met, to have met a nice, decent person who wanted to take care of her, we thanked God."

Soon, Kristin enrolled at San Diego State University. Her professors later said described Rossum as a stellar student with one going so far as to describe her as "among the most promising students" he had "ever taught."

Everyone who knew her believed she was happy. She was earning straight As and in 1998, she graduated cum laude (with honors). She got a job at San Diego Medical Examiner's office as a toxicologist.

Constance would later testify, "Our old Kristin was back," and she thanked God and de Villers – in that order – for the change.

Storybook Love?

Everyone who knew them described Kristin and Greg as the perfect couple. Constance Rossum testified later that when they were together they were "like a couple of lovebirds." When they announced their engagement, nobody was surprised.

However, as is often the case, outward appearances did not accurately represent reality. There was a layer of tension beneath the surface of de Villers and Rossum's storybook love affair. Kristin's closest friends knew that she had a hard time staying faithful and monogamous.

According to prosecutor's later, Kristin actually maintained a "graphically flirtatious" correspondence with a former boyfriend and at least one other man during at least some portion of her relationship with de Villers. Rossum even went to her mother only a month before she was supposed to walk down the aisle and broke down in tears as she told her mother that she wanted to cancel the wedding.

Constance Rossum considered her daughter's outburst to be cold feet, pre-wedding jitters that would pass. After all, Greg de Villers was the man who led her out of the darkness of addiction and Constance could not see how Kristin could possibly want to end the relationship.

She would soon tell the court, "I gave her the wrong counsel, I'm afraid."

The wedding was spectacular. The video shows a smiling and laughing Kristin Rossum, now Kristin de Villers, dancing with her new husband and looking happy. As for de Villers, he is recorded on that video saying, "Kristin is the most wonderful person I've ever met. I just can't wait to spend the rest of my life with her."

Only seven months after the wedding, however, Kristin Rossum told her mother that she felt "trapped like a bird in a cage." It was January 2000 and Kristin's journal shows that she had begun souring on her marriage only a couple of months after the wedding.

Greg de Villers did not show any sign that he felt the same or even knew of his wife's misgivings and doubt. Conversely, his brother

Jerome later testified that Greg was ecstatically happy and never spoke of anything even smacking of marital discord. Even his colleagues at a genetics research firm where de Villers worked, described him as happily married and devoted to his wife. Some even went so far as to describe Greg de Villers as "sickeningly in love with his wife."

Friends of Greg de Villers said that he was often talking about his plans for their future together. He bragged about his wife's accomplishments, both big and small, and often spoke of starting a family. One friend remembers him saying that he wanted "all girls who were as beautiful and smart as Kristin."

At the same time, his adored wife was painting a much grimmer portrait of her marriage and her husband. She often complained to colleagues and friends about Greg, saying that he was moody, controlling, and domineering. Later, in an interview with "48 Hours," Kristin said, "Greg became very, very clinging... I tried to pull away and have some sort of independence."

An email sent to her brother Brent only 11 months after the wedding showed how she truly felt. She wrote, "I should have trusted my own instincts and called off the wedding. Now I'm stuck with the heavy realization that I married the wrong person."

A New Love Affair

Not long after Kristin Rossum sent that email to her brother, she met Dr. Michael Robertson. Newly hired as Chief Toxicologist at the San Diego Medical Examiner's office, Robertson was Kristin's immediate supervisor and she began spending large amounts of time with him.

Soon, they were spending time together outside of work. Kristin found danger and excitement in her passionate affair with her handsome, Australian doctor – who was also married. Her husband – and the problems she seemed to have with him – disappeared from Kristin's consideration and soon she was talking with friends outside of her colleagues about the wonderful new man in her life who she described as "a big hunk of an Australian guy."

By early May, Rossum was receiving inappropriate emails and notes from her boss. A search of her desk later turned up love notes and IOUs for things such as "a night of lovemaking" from Robertson. Coworkers later reported that Robertson was often seen sauntering into work with a bouquet of flowers that would soon end up on Rossum's desk.

In June, according to court records, Kristin Rossum had given her lover a gift. A book titled "52 Invitations To Great Sex" she had inscribed on the inside cover, "Well, sweetheart, together we'll enjoy a lifetime of passion."

When asked later, Rossum said, "I felt like I was in love. It was very romantic, very exciting, very passionate."

In August of 2000, Kristin turned to her best friend, Melissa Prager. Prager later told the court that he friend confided in her that she was madly in love with Robertson but was "terrified" by the idea of telling Greg she wanted a divorce.

In October 2000, Greg de Villers was still telling his friends, family, co-workers, and anyone else who would listen about his love for his wife and his plans for their future. His brother Jerome later told the court that around Halloween, Greg was talking about his excitement over taking his future children with Kristin out to trick or treat.

However, Kristin Rossum had reached a conclusion about her marriage. She told her close friends that she was looking for an apartment and planned to leave her husband.

'Til Death Do Us Part

It is unclear how de Villers learned of his wife's infidelity and plan to leave him. Rossum has always claimed that she told Greg de Villers about the affair and that her admission launched a spiraling depression in her husband.

According to Kristin Rossum, she told her husband about Robertson and he demanded the man's phone number. When Kristin supplied the number (although why she would is uncertain), de Villers called her boss and lover and demanded that he break off their relationship.

There is no court record of a response to this demand by Robertson. However, the relationship continued.

Authorities, however, have a very different set of circumstances in mind for how Greg discovered Kristin's infidelity.

They maintain that de Villers found out about the affair on accident in the fall of 2000. This was after Kristin and Robertson were sent to Milwaukee together to attend a toxicology conference. According to court records, despite being booked into separate hotels – likely due to rumors in the office about their relationship – the duo rented their own room together and spent several nights from September 30 to October 7 together in that room.

A coworker saw Kristin at the conference during the week and noted that she was no longer wearing her wedding ring.

One of the conferences that Rossum and Robertson attended in Milwaukee was on the deadly effects of fentanyl. Fentanyl is a clear, odorless narcotic that is 100 times stronger than morphine. It is generally administered to cancer patients whose pain is not eased by other means. It is so potent that it only takes a few drops to kill.

The seminar also discussed the fact that the drug is so rarely prescribed and used that most medical examiner's offices do not test for it. Both Rossum and Robertson were well aware of the fact that their office did not test for fentanyl.

During the three years that Rossum had worked in the San Diego Medical Examiner's office, only seven cases of death by overdose had involved fentanyl. She had seen 15 patches and 1 vial of the drug in a powder form. It was Rossum's job to log and track the drugs in her logbook. It was Robertson's job to hold the key to the cabinet those substances was then stored in.

These were facts that seemed innocuous at the time but would soon hold a more serious meaning.

Returning to Old Ways

Only a day or two after returning from Milwaukee, Rossum sent de Villers an email telling him that she was taking three different prescription drugs "to help with the severe anxiety I've been experiencing as a result of our relationship. You've hurt me beyond repair."

Not only was Kristin taking prescription medications, she had fallen back into her addiction to meth. After some of the drugs went missing from her office, Robertson admitted later that he found traces of the drug in her desk and rather than turning his girlfriend in, he flushed the drugs down the toilet. Then he covered for her with his superiors.

Once again, Kristin Rossum has done something bad. Once again, somebody shields her from the ramifications of her actions. Once again, there are no consequences for Kristin's bad actions.

Severing Ties

By early November 2000, Rossum was ready to end her relationship with de Villers. She insisted she wanted only a "trial separation."

She later told detectives that de Villers literally collapsed when she told him she was leaving him. She claimed that he lay in bed for days afterward and would not communicate with her. She later told the court, "It was painful for me, too, to see someone you love hurt so much." She still never owned up to the fact that it was her own actions that caused her husband that pain.

On November 6, 2000, just after 9:15 pm, Kristin Rossum called 991.

She claimed that her husband was unresponsive and that she was doing CPR to try and revive him. When paramedics arrived, however, they found Rossum on the phone in the living room. Her husband was lying lifeless on their bed.

Gregory de Villers lay dead in his La Jolla bedroom with rose petals covering his chest. Besides his lifeless head lay a copy of his wedding picture ... less than two years old. Nearby on the floor lay a crumpled love letter from the dashing Australian doctor that was his wife's boss and lover. Beside that was his wife's discarded diary, open to an entry that she had left confiding that she felt her marriage was the biggest mistake of her life.

For all intents and purposes, it looked like a suicide. His distraught widow claimed that Greg had learned that her affair with Robertson was still happening.

However, de Villers' brother Jerome adamantly refused to accept that his brother had committed suicide. The entire de Villers family demanded an investigation. Still, the San Diego police were hesitant to open an investigation.

The Truth and Nothing but the Truth

Their opinion quickly changed and authorities soon came to suspect Kristin Rossum, de Villers' 26-year-old blonde beauty of a wife. They believed that she had used her knowledge as a toxicologist and the information that she had gleaned from working in the medical examiner's office to poison her husband.

Due to concerns over a conflict of interest, de Villers' autopsy was outsourced to another lab in Los Angeles. That lab is one of the few in the country that tests for fentanyl. They found 7 times the lethal dose of fentanyl in de Villers' system.

Two weeks after de Villers' death, the San Diego police brought Kristin Rossum in for interrogation. She reiterated to police that her husband had been extremely depressed.

According to Kristin Rossum's story, on the Thursday before de Villers' death, they struggled over a letter that she had sticking out of her back pocket. In her account, de Villers' attempted to grab the letter from her pocket and knocked her to the ground to wrest it from her. She claimed that it was the first time she had been afraid of her husband.

When he had the letter, as Rossum's story goes, he held it out and threatened to take it to his wife's office and expose the affair as well as her reoccurring meth addiction. She took the letter and shredded it but de Villers pieced it back together.

In court, Rossum's parents described the night, two days before de Villers' death, when they went over to visit the couple for dinner. Ralph Rossum testified that de Villers seemed to be deeply depressed, "a man spiraling down."

Kristin Rossum's father continued to describe how de Villers had drunk heavily that night. He drank wine and gin until his father in law had to tell him to lower his voice. Constance Rossum described Greg de Villers' voice as "fraught with melodrama" as he spoke at length about the dozen red roses that he had given to Kristin for her birthday a few days earlier.

She testified that he seemed depressed, agitated, and particularly obsessed with the fact that all but one had died and shed its petals. In a TV interview, she gave months after the death, Rossum stated, "He was making a big deal of the last rose standing. I think he was just making a statement that he knew our relationship was over."

Things rapidly spiraled from that point on. Police learned that Rossum had relapsed and was using meth again.

On June 25, 2001 – 7 months after Greg de Villers' death – his wife was arrested on charges of First Degree Murder. She spent over six months in jail and then on January 4, 2002, her parents posted $1.25 million for bail.

During the trial, the prosecution contended that she killed her husband to keep him from telling her bosses that she was having an affair with Robertson and that she was stealing meth from the office. They presented evidence that she had the knowledge about fentanyl to use it, access to the drug (remember the missing fentanyl from her office), and the motive to kill her husband.

On November 12, 2002, Kristin Rossum was found guilty of first-degree murder.

Exactly one month later on December 12, she was sentenced to life in prison without the chance of parole. She was transferred from the San Diego jail to the Central California Women's Facility in Chowchilla California – the largest women's correctional facility in the United States.

Distant Repercussions

In 2006, the de Villers family filed a lawsuit against Rossum and San Diego County for wrongful death. They were asking for $50 million but on March 25, 2006, a San Diego jury ordered Rossum to pay more than $100 million in punitive damages to the de Villers family. The same judge ordered San Diego County to pay $1.5 million.

According to the de Villers' lawyer John Gomez, the punitive damages awarded in this case are the most assessed against an individual defendant in California history. The jury apparently awarded double what the de Villers' family was asking for due to the estimation that Rossum could make $60 million from selling the rights to her story.

The judge later lowered the awarded amounts to $10 million in punitive damages and $4.5 million in a compensatory award.

In September of 2010, a 3-judge panel of the 9th US Circuit Court of Appeals ruled that Rossum's lawyers should have challenged the prosecutions assertion that she poisoned her husband with fentanyl by demanding their own tests. Due to this, the panel ordered a San Diego federal court to hold a hearing into whether the defense's error could have affected the trial's outcome.

On September 13, 2011, the US Court of Appeals withdrew its opinion and replaced it with a one-paragraph statement that denied Rossum's petition.

Conclusion

Kristin Rossum will spend the rest of her life behind bars. She has exhausted her state appeals and the federal courts denied her petition to be heard.

Her contention remains that her husband killed himself. She further believes that he did it the way that he did to point the finger of guilt at her. She vehemently insists that she did not kill her husband.

At one point, Kristin Rossum even suggested that her lover the handsome Australian doctor might have killed her husband. He knew about de Villers' threat to expose them before his death and had access to the fentanyl.

For his part, Robertson returned to Brisbane, Australia only one month after de Villers' death under the excuse that he had to care for his ailing mother. In September of 2013, the San Diego Reader reported that prosecutors filed a criminal complaint against Robertson in 2006 charging him with one count of conspiracy to obstruct justice.

If he returned to the US, Robertson could face up to three years in prison. In 2001, Robertson was named as an "unindicted co-conspirator" in Rossum's trial.

As of 2014, Robertson was running a forensic consulting business in Brisbane.

Kristin Rossum, the sweet spoiled only daughter of college professors, who was never held accountable for her actions as she grew up will spend the rest of her days within the walls of the largest women's correctional facility in the US. She is finally going to have to answer for what she has done.

BLACK WIDOW LYDA TRUEBLOOD

JESSI DILLARD

A true "black widow"

Death followed Lyda Trueblood everywhere she went. At first glance, it may have seemed that the young woman was facing a run of bad luck – but as the run continued, suspicions began to arise.

Northeast of Kansas City, in the small town of Keytesville, Missouri, a true "black widow" was born on October 16, 1892. Over the course of her life, Lyda Anna Mae Trueblood took on seven married names, and is most well-known as Lyda Southard. However, Idaho remembers her as Lady Bluebeard – the state's first female serial killer.

"She swept the men of her choice off their feet – courted them so persistently that they could not escape," said V. H. Ormsby, a deputy sheriff from Twin Falls, Idaho. Ormsby was one of the officers who arrested Trueblood in Honolulu for the death of her fourth husband.

By the age of 27, Trueblood had already killed six people, including her own daughter. However, she would only be convicted of one murder – the poisoning of her fourth husband, Edward Meyer, in 1921.

"The marital experiences of the one-time Missouri country town girl eclipses even those of fiction. Ten years ago, while still in her teens, she was attending Sunday school and enjoying the popularity that goes with being a village belle."

Described as "pudgy faced and plain of figure," Trueblood still caught the eye of Robert Dooley, whose family was close with Trueblood's. Some said Trueblood was the most popular girl at her high school, claiming she had an "indefinable something, a spark giving off a light that draws men, by physiological and chemical attraction."

"They wasn't so wealthy, just so-so," said Mrs. Larrabee Hanson, who lived near the Trueblood family. "But they were all church-going people, devout and clean-living. (Trueblood) went to church every Sunday without fail."

A magazine writer, Alan Jaffe, who detailed Trueblood's history for a profile in *Argosy* magazine in 1957, said men "hung around her like flies about a honey pot." In fact, when Trueblood finally left her childhood home and moved to Twin Falls, Robert Dooley followed – and the two were married there in 1912, when she was only 21.

A promise of the future

"They had a perfectly normal relationship," said Mychel Matthews with the Twin Falls County Historical Museum. "They appeared to be just like the rest of the residents around town."

With the security of their future family in mind, the newlyweds decided to take out an insurance policy on Robert and his brother, Edward. If either died, the survivor would inherit $1,000 – with an equal amount going to Trueblood. And by August 1915, the couple was $2,000 richer. Edward Dooley had fallen ill and had died after just a few days – typhoid, the doctors said.

"There was nothing suspicious about the death," Matthews said. "It was ruled as food poisoning or typhoid."

As Edward lay dying, Trueblood convinced her husband to revise his insurance policy – for the family's protection, she argued. A new policy was drafted for Robert and his wife, stating that if either died, the surviving spouse would receive $2,000.

Just one month later, Robert Dooley followed in his brother's footsteps – succumbing to typhoid in a similar fashion. Trueblood, however, had begun to build herself a substantial nest egg. Only six weeks after losing her husband, Trueblood's infant daughter, Laura Marie, "drank from a contaminated well," according to reports – leaving the widow lonely and desperate for companionship.

Since accidental poisonings did occasionally occur in rural areas, and epidemics – particularly typhoid – were rampant during that time, the deaths of the Dooleys were only briefly investigated by authorities.

"Little children died all the time, at that period of history," Matthews said. "She probably got a lot of sympathy, 'oh, that poor woman. She's lost her daughter, her husband, all to this stomach flu.'"

Trueblood endured a brief but mandatory period of mourning after losing her family, but soon struck up a relationship with a waiter at her favorite Twin Falls restaurant. William McHaffie married Trueblood just two years after the loss of her first husband and only child, and the couple immediately sought an insurance policy for William. Trueblood was named as William's only beneficiary, to receive $5,000 if anything was to happen to him.

The couple moved to Hardin, Montana, and only a year after they married, William died of "influenza." According to his friends and customers, William had always been a robust, healthy man – and the speed and depth of his sudden illness shocked them.

"Lyda Trublood was very careful," said crime author Diane Fanning. "She waited until they actually got sick – then, it was easier to believe that they had died of an illness. Everybody thought it was something he ate that finally did him in, but all that it was, really, was Lyda Trueblood."

Unfortunately for Trueblood, however, William had failed to pay the second premium on his insurance policy, letting it lapse. Trueblood received nothing for her efforts. Days after her late husband's funeral, Trueblood sold all her property and disappeared.

Moving on

After relocating to Denver, Trueblood managed to ensnare another victim – a farm machinery salesman she had met during her previous marriage to William. In fact, William had told friends that after he'd come to their door in an attempt to make a sale, Trueblood had seemed "struck" by him – and neighbours reported that the happy couple had even started fighting more after that.

Trueblood married Harlan Lewis in March of 1919, and took him with her back to Montana. The couple settled in Billings, and only one month later, Harlan took out a $10,000 life insurance policy. According to Matthews, the larger policies are an indication that

Trueblood was manipulating the men in order to receive greater payouts.

"(Trueblood) was motivated by one thing, and one thing only - greed," said former FBI profiler Candice Delong. "She wanted money."

By mid-July, just three months after the wedding, disaster had struck. After falling ill to a sudden case "ptomaine poisoning," Harlan left Trueblood a widow for the third time – and this time, the cheque came through. After cashing out the estate, Trueblood disappeared again. Instead of heading somewhere new, however, Trueblood decided to return to Idaho.

Under the name of Lyda McHaffie, Trueblood checked into the Rogerson Hotel in Twin Falls in May 1919, and found herself a job at the Grille Café on Main Avenue. Business at the café picked up immediately, reports claim, and the foreman of Ira Perrine's Blue Lake Ranch, Edward Meyer, started visiting the restaurant regularly.

"Folks couldn't help noticing that the air sort of shimmered when (Trueblood's) eyes met Ed's," wrote Jaffe in his profile. "And that the ham he got was thicker, the eggs sunnier than those served other patrons."

The very next month, Trueblood moved to Pocatello, Idaho, where she married Edward Meyer and settled on a ranch.

"She rigged herself out fit to kill, bought a long mink coat and a closed car. Everybody in town was talking about the way she ran around to dances," said Ormsby. "She talked around town that she wasn't in love with Ed, but she wanted a home, and she said that sometime she might learn to love him."

Although she had started going by the name "Anna McHaffie," Trueblood showed no other signs of leaving her past life behind her. She applied for an insurance policy in Edward's name the day after the wedding, in the amount of $10,000 – however, the policy was not approved, and reasons were never clarified. It's possible that insurance companies were beginning to wise up to the run of bad luck Trueblood had encountered.

Suspicious situation

Only two weeks after the couple had wed, on August 25, Edward took ill. Doctors at the hospital claimed he had an excellent chance of recovery, but he was dead by September 7.

"She didn't wait for him to get sick," said Matthews. "Maybe she grew impatient, and that was probably the mistake she made in all of this."

Trueblood's previous husbands had been fairly low-key, unlikely to attract attention despite the unbelievable series of coincidences that had resulted in their deaths – and Trueblood's subsequent insurance claims. Edward Meyer, however, was a different case. As a prominent figure in Twin Falls, Edward had dealings with many of the leading business and farm people in the region – including the Twin Falls county sheriff.

"The townsfolk weren't just satisfied," Ormsby said. "They started a lot of talk, and the insurance company held up payment on the policy. The matter got into politics and folks wanted to know what the candidates for sheriff would do about (Trueblood)."

When traces of arsenic were discovered during a routine post-mortem examination, detectives finally brought the widow in for questioning.

"The investigation was just getting underway when the woman disappeared," stated an article published in the New York Times on May 13, 1921. "Detectives traced her to Los Angeles, and kept track of her while the bodies of the two (Dooleys), the infant daughter, and McHaffie were exhumed and portions of the viscera were sent to chemists."

Edward Meyer's death had become somewhat of a political issue in the 1920 campaign for sheriff, and potential candidates were asked how they planned to handle the case. The current sheriff passed the case to a "remarkable" deputy, Virgin Ormsby – and the investigation would be virtually his only assignment for months.

"After she left for California, the town got more dissatisfied than ever, and in January, I was assigned to the case," Ormsby said. "I've had the bodies of the men dissatisfied and examined – three chemists each working separately reported to me that they found arsenic. I interviewed the doctors who attended the husbands and obtained statements from them that enabled me to build a strong case against her."

Ormsby even discovered that a relative of Trueblood's first husband and brother-in-law had been studying the suspicious deaths in his family. A chemist named Earl Dooley had already begun to consider the possibility that Robert and Edward Dooley had been poisoned with arsenic – and according to Fanning, his suspicions led him to investigate the scene of Trueblood's most recent victim.

After taking samples from Edward Meyer's vomit in the sand, Earl had them tested.

"Sure enough, he found arsenic – and when that happened, he went to a doctor to get it confirmed in another lab," Fanning said. "It was definitely arsenic."

Mounting evidence

Police first determined that the Dooley brothers had been poisoned, as well as Trueblood's own child. Officers in Montana started investigating the cases of Harlan Lewis and William McHaffie, intrigued by the seemingly impossible coincidences that had led Trueblood to make so many insurance claims. Trueblood, meanwhile, was busy seducing her fifth husband, Paul Southard, in Los Angeles – while prosecutor Frank L. Stephen started building a case against her back in Twin Falls.

While working odd jobs, saving her money, and reportedly describing herself as a nurse, Trueblood managed to convince Paul to propose. The two were married in November of 1920. Although Paul, who served as a seaman in the navy, claimed he needed no additional insurance coverage beyond typical provisions, Ormsby learned that a policy had in fact been taken out on Chief Petty Officer Paul Southard – with Trueblood named as the beneficiary.

Shortly after they were wed, Paul was transferred from Los Angeles to Pearl Harbour, and his new bride joined him in Hawaii. Ormsby was in hot pursuit, having tracked Trueblood with the help of California law enforcement. Officers in Honolulu received a warrant for Trueblood's arrest in May 1921. She was picked up on May 12 to return to Boise, Idaho, for her trial – with her husband Paul at her side.

"She's been a mighty good wife to me," said Paul, who refused to believe the charges, "and I don't care if she married ten men before, and they all died. That wouldn't make her a murderess."

Although tabloids had already started running headlines about the gruesome tale, labelling Trueblood catchy names like "Lethal Lyda" or "The Arsenic Widow," Trueblood maintained her innocence as she and Paul prepared to catch the *Matsonia* out of Honolulu. Some reports claimed she was acting "like any lucky vacationer about to embark on an ocean cruise," her neck heavy with flowered leis.

"I am entirely innocent, and I look forward to the trip with optimism," Trueblood said in a brief statement to the press. "I am anxious to get back to Twin Falls and face my accusers."

At the jail, Trueblood finally granted an interview to reporter Hazel Pedlar Faulkner, with the San Francisco Examiner. Pedlar Faulkner described the accused as "dainty, friendly, and refined" – not exactly the picture of a "sinister murderer," she said.

"I have been nervous because of my imprisonment and the unnecessary disgrace to my husband," Pedlar Faulkner quotes Trueblood as saying. "I know as well as anything that I can clear myself. The evidence gathered against me is purely circumstantial. Their work is to prove the charges, and that will not be easy because of the documents I hold."

Trueblood claimed that her husbands had died because she was a "typhoid carrier," and even stated that she had nothing to do with the large life insurance policies her late husbands had all secured before their untimely deaths.

"Life insurance was no object to me," stated Trueblood in Pedlar Faulkner's interview. "I have had enough money. And what insurance my husbands carried were business propositions they took out without regard to me or without consulting me, generally."

Before leaving San Francisco to bring Trueblood back to Boise, Ormsby and his wife, Nellie, took the accused for one last night on the town. After having dinner at a restaurant and strolling through a downtown shopping district, the Ormsbys and their charge attended a vaudeville show at the Orpheum Theatre.

Although Trueblood was trying to remain under the radar, a San Francisco Chronicle reporter recognized her – and wrote about her activities the next morning.

"With the grim specters of four dead husbands, a brother-in-law, and her infant baby hovering near her, while the accusing finger of the law points at her and charges murder, Mrs. Lyda Eva Southard, psychological enigma, calmly spent yesterday seeing the sights of San Francisco," read Herb Westen's article in the San Francisco Call and Post.

"She smiles, a trifle shyly perhaps, but a bored light creeps around her eyes as if to her it is all a tedious legal jumble, which will steal precious hours from her pursuit of happiness."

Up to the jury
Despite Trueblood's denial of the charges, the state contended that she'd fed Edward Meyer, her fourth husband, hefty doses of arsenic extracted from flypaper. Trueblood denied it and the state presented further evidence – largely circumstantial, but it was still enough for a conviction.

The trial, which started on October 3 and lasted six weeks, received attention nation-wide. At the time, it would become the longest criminal trial in history. Witnesses were called from Missouri, Montana, Tennessee, and California – a total of 182 named to appear, but not all were called to the stand.

Prosecutor Stephen tried desperately to bring in Buddy Thornberg to testify against Trueblood – a reporter for the Daily News in Twin Falls who had come close to marrying Trueblood shortly before she snagged Edward Meyer. He'd met the widow at the café, and she had swept him off his feet. According to reports, Thornberg had told his friends he would be marrying the "rich widow from Montana," and – on her advice – he was considering taking out an additional private insurance policy on top of the $10,000 government policy he already had in place.

After his friends managed to convince him to not follow through with a marriage, however, Thornberg had ended his relationship with Trueblood and was presumed to have moved to Washington – never to be heard from again.

An article claimed that "every session of the trial found the court auditorium filled to capacity, principally by women and girls." Another report claimed the trail was, "draggy," and "rather technical – arsenic versus typhoid, laboratory tests versus the official death certificate. This certificate, giving typhoid as the cause of death, was more or less (Trueblood's) sole defense."

The whole case presented against Trueblood suggested that she didn't particularly love her husband, and could have – and likely did – poison him. Not only that, she took out insurance on his life, and fled immediately after his death.

According to Ormsby, a visit to the McHaffies' home in Montana had uncovered evidence to back up this theory. He'd discovered a "large quantity" of cut-up flypaper containing arsenic in the basement, with residue of arsenic in a pot Trueblood had likely used to boil the poison out – before serving it to her husband in tainted food.

"(Trueblood) went about her killing very deliberately," Fanning said. "She bought out everything the store had in flypaper. It was obvious that she wanted to have a permanent supply on hand."

An article published in the New York Times on October 9, 1921 stated that under the questioning of Prosecuting Attorney Frank Stephen, Dr E. F. Roberbaugh, state chemist, confirmed the presence of arsenic poison in the body of Edward Meyer when he examined the body in April of that year.

"The witness testified he found .05 milligrams of poison in five grams of a specimen of several internal organs and .10 milligrams in a ten-gram quantity of the specimen," the article read. "The witness said the distribution of poison throughout the system was not equal and he estimated that a little less than five grains of poison probably was contained in Meyer's body."

He added that the findings "virtually duplicated" those obtained immediately after Edward Meyer's death in September, 1920.

The state requested permission to introduce further evidence relating to the deaths of Trueblood's other husbands, and the judge ruled the testimony admissible. While physicians did, in some instances, contradict testimony of other expert witnesses on the question of cause of death, analysis made by three separate chemists agreed that poison was present in all bodies exhumed.

"She poisoned their food, and over time, the arsenic would build up," said Fanning. "Most of the death certificates all said some sort of stomach ailment."

After a deliberation of twenty-three hours, the jury came back with a verdict on November 4, 1921. Trueblood was found guilty of second-degree murder. Speculation was that the jury had "blanched" at the thought of hanging a woman, but there was no doubt that she had done it. Even her husband, Paul Southard, filed for divorce after watching the trial.

"Lyda Trueblood was a classic black widow," Delong said. "And she did it for money."

According to an article in the November 5, 1921 issue of the Sacramento Union, Trueblood showed "no sign of feeling," and didn't even raise her eyes from the floor as the verdict was read. This was typical of Trueblood's attitude throughout the trial, however.

"On the stand, the accused woman maintained an unperturbed attitude throughout a long grilling by the prosecution, which failed to adduce any important admissions from her," the article stated.

Only eight years after Trueblood's incarceration, Ormsby suffered a paralytic stroke and died in his wife's arms. His obituary ran on the front page of the December 30, 1929 edition of the Twin Falls Times – and flowers were delivered to his funeral, sent from a Lyda Southard.

A "break for freedom"

Still, the guilty verdict and the sentence of at least ten years in prison wasn't enough to keep Trueblood from seducing men.

"She proved that no prison walls can hold her, and made her escape from the Idaho State Penitentiary by fascinating, as did Milady, a prison guard, who is believed to have rigged up for her an ingenious ladder of plumbers' pipes and torn blankets and garden hose," read an article published in the October 25, 1931 issue of the Salt Lake Tribune. "This guard, however, died before (Trueblood) made her break for freedom."

According to the article, Trueblood had already served ten years of her sentence and was eligible for parole when she made her great escape on May 4, 1931. The ladder, fashioned for her by prison guard Jack Watkins, had been buried for months beneath the prison walls. Watkins had also provided Trueblood with a saw, which she used to remove a bar from her cell window.

"The escape itself was dramatic," the article continued. "Women inmates, evidently under the spell of the woman, who could fascinate those of her own sex as well as men, staged a party and played the phonograph and sang while she was gaining her way to liberty."

Trueblood ran right into the arms of David Minton. Minton, an ex-convict himself, had fallen under Trueblood's spell while he was still behind bars. After he helped Trueblood escape from prison, she'd ended the relationship. Leaving him alive was a mistake, however – enraged, Minton went to the police and told them they could find Trueblood in Topeka, Kansas.

This, however, was not before a nation-wide manhunt was organized to attempt to locate Trueblood, who was described by Warden R. E. Thomas of the Idaho State Penitentiary as "one of the most dangerous criminals at large."

"Some man will probably pay with his life in agony and death before this ruthless woman can again be brought to justice," he said. "That she is the modern 'Mrs. Bluebeard' is certain."

In fact, before the police found her in Kansas, Trueblood had managed to swindle another man into marrying her. Harry Whitlock, who later described Trueblood as a "model wife," was shocked when the police showed up looking for her. The relationship had begun when Trueblood, calling herself "Fern," had started doing housekeeping work for Whitlock – and she had suggested he take out a $20,000 life insurance policy, but it hadn't been purchased before she asked him for some travel money and took off.

Fifteen months after her escape, Trueblood was returned to Boise – with her marriage to Whitlock annulled.

Back in prison, Trueblood continued to seduce her prey. This time, she set her sights on George Rudd, a prison warden. She managed to convince him to grant her special privileges – frequent day trip to a local resort, visitation to see her sick mother, and even transportation to Boise to see movies. However, when authorities discovered that he'd been treating Trueblood to these privileges, Rudd was forced to resign from his position.

Free at last

Finally, Trueblood was paroled from prison on October 3, 1941, and fully pardoned only one year later.

"I think they figured that she had lost most of her good looks and charm, and was no longer a menace to society," Matthews said.

After spending a few years living with her sister, Blanche Quigley, in Nyssa, Oregon, Trueblood returned to her family's farm at Twin Falls – but the local townspeople and even her relatives weren't pleased to see her.

A few months later, Trueblood left for Provo, Utah, where no one knew her, and pulled together the funds to purchase a small secondhand shop. There, she married her seventh husband, Hal Shaw. However, once Shaw's children discovered who she was and learned about her unsavory past, he vanished – leaving her to move to Salt Lake City, where she worked for several years as a housekeeper and waitress.

"You wonder, did (the husbands) ever suspect that it was not a natural illness that was making them suffer in agony," Fanning said. "We can only hope that they never understood what was really happening."

Trueblood died of a heart attack on February 5, 1958 in Salt Lake City. Her body remains at Sunset Memorial Park in Twin Falls, Idaho, where she was buried as Anna E. Shaw. Still, some report seeing a ghost bearing Trueblood's likeness haunting the halls of the Idaho prison to this day – the prison's most notorious inmate, maintaining a presence even after her death.

"When she finally died, it was from a heart attack," Fanning said. "It's amazing to think that (Trueblood) actually had a heart."

BLACK WIDOW : THE TRUE STORY OF MARGARET RUDIN

88

BRIANNA VALDES

Margaret Rudin, dubbed the Black Widow of Las Vegas, went on trial on February 26, 2001 for the murder of her fifth husband, real estate king Ronald Rudin. After a lengthy, chaotic trial and her defense claiming that involvement in illegal activities resulted in Ron's death, the jury found her guilty on May 2, 2001. In August, the court sentenced Margaret Rudin to life in prison with the possibility of parole in 20 years.

According to reports, Ron Rudin went missing about a week before Christmas in '94. He paid a visit to wife Margaret Rudin's antique shop, in the same plaza as his real estate business. Officials said that Margaret Rudin did not report Ron missing until a few days after he disappeared. She told police she thought nothing of it at first because, aside from Ron being upset with her after an argument, he seemed like his usual self.

About a month after Ron disappeared, a couple of civilians stumbled upon human remain near Lake Mohave in Nevada. Police found ashes and fragments of bones in the burn pile. However, the skull, which was inches away, remained mostly intact. It had at least four bullet holes, which forensics later matched to a .22 caliber weapon. Police made two trips to the house, and on the second visit, they found blood on the walls, photographs and items removed from the house including a mattress and carpet. However, though the police suspected that Margaret Rudin killed her husband, the evidence up to that point was circumstantial at best.

A year and a half year later, a diver found a .22 caliber gun with a built-in silencer in Lake Mead. This was the same gun Ron Rudin reported missing about six years before his death. When officials tested the gun in the forensics lab, the ammo matched the rounds found in Ron Rudin's skull. Police determined that the .22 was the murder weapon, and, with this new piece of evidence added to the other circumstantial clues they had, charged Margaret Rudin with the murder of her husband. However, Margaret left town before they indicted and arrested her, and she stayed out of sight for over two years.

Almost a year after the diver found the gun that allegedly killed Ron Rudin, police finally indicted Margaret Rudin.

Authorities finally apprehended Margaret Rudin in 1999. Someone who saw her picture and story on the T.V. show "America's Most Wanted" called and reported seeing her in a small town in Massachusetts.

Police used a pizza delivery person to help them capture Margaret. They borrowed the person's uniform and an empty pizza box, and barged in the house when her male companion opened the door. According to some reports, they found her cowering in the bathroom.

Margaret Rudin was born Margaret Lee Frost in Memphis, Tennessee on May 31, 1943. She said that she and her family never lived in one place for very long, and that she and her two sisters constantly changed schools.

"I didn't grow up any place. We were constantly moving, you know, like, I transferred schools 22 different times, um, before I graduated high school. I lived in 15 states in 15 years. I never had a hometown."

Margaret said that her father was strict and dominating, and that he rarely showed affection to her or her sisters.

Both Margaret and Ron were married four times before they met at the First Church of Religious Science in Las Vegas. They married on September 11, 1987.

Margaret's mother, Eloise Frost, stood behind her daughter throughout the entire trial. She never believed Margaret capable of murder.

"I want to live long enough to see Margaret pronounced innocent, because she is innocent."

Margaret Rudin's daughter, Kristina Mason firmly believed that her mother was innocent. She said her childhood was a good one, and that the mother with whom she grew up was not a murderer.

"She's just a wonderful person and I'm proud to say she's my mother."

The court sentenced Margaret Rudin in September 2001. Although she received life in a medium security facility, plus a year for planting the bugs in her husband's office, they also added that she would be eligible for parole in 2011. She began preparing, and petitioning, for her appeal, carefully heeding the filing deadlines.

80-year-old Eloise cried when Margaret was convicted, saying that now she may never see her daughter again.

Kristina Mason burst into tears.

"I'm so disappointed."

Ronald Rudin seemed to predict his own death, or at least his murder. Months before he went missing, he had his will changed, with specific instructions for investigators to follow in the event that he died under suspicious circumstances.

"In the event my death is caused by violent means [for example gunshot, knife or a violent automobile accident] extraordinary steps be taken in investigating the true cause of the death. Should said death be caused directly or indirectly by a beneficiary of my estate, said beneficiary shall be totally excluded from my estate and/or any trusts I may have in existence."

Although most of Nevada's case against Margaret was circumstantial, authorities say there were a few things that seemed suspicious to them from the beginning. First, Margaret herself admitted that her marriage to Ron was less than ideal. She told police that they often argued about her work schedule. Later, when authorities discovered that she had planted listening devices in Ron Rudin's home office, she also admitted that she suspected that Ron was having an affair, and upon eavesdropping on a phone conversation, discovered proof to back her suspicions.

Jimmy Vacarro, a Vegas detective, confirmed that the Las Vegas police believed without a doubt that Margaret Rudin was responsible for Ron's murder.

"We know there was this real rocky roller-coaster relationship between Margaret Rudin and her husband... [It took] Margaret two days to file a missing persons report and that she did so only after Ron's coworkers informed police first...Generally speaking, the spouse is missing, the wife's the one reporting it."

Second, officials say that Margaret waited a few days before reporting Ron missing, even though his employees at his real estate company were concerned and investigating as soon as he did not show up that Monday morning.

Margaret Rudin offered a logical explanation to her hesitation to bring in police. She said she thought little of it at first because they had another fight and he left angry, which was common for Ron. She also said that, aside from Ron being upset with her after an argument, he seemed like his usual self.

"He seemed ok. He does not seem upset. He had, had been a little peeved at me over the weekend because I had to work all the time... "Well, I thought nothing of it because, you know, maybe he did get peeved... and maybe he did decide to go out for awhile... maybe he did go to, you know... wherever."

Margaret made a point of mentioning her previous marriages in one of her interviews.

"I don't have a history of staying with somebody if I'm really unhappy. I have a history of divorcing... There was problems. He was a difficult person at times, but yes, I did love him..."

Margaret said Ron also drank quite a bit after just a few months of marriage. However, she told reporters that she was not mad about the alcohol or the other women, even when Su Lyles, a close friend and a former employee of Mr. Rudin's, testified that in the fall of 1993, their relationship became more intimate. At least twice, she said, they had discussed their feelings for each other over the telephone during calls made from his office.

"You know why? It is because 99 percent of the men that I have ever had in my life had affairs. Ninety percent of men do, you might as well expect it."

Margaret admitted that, although the affairs wounded her, she loved her husband and desperately wanted to work out things with him.

Police grew even more suspicious when they discovered that Margaret hired a man named Augustine Lovato to help her remove some dirty carpet and furniture from the master bedroom. She then renovated the bedroom she shared with her husband into an office while Ron was still missing.

Lovato testified that the mattress and carpet he removed from the Rudin's home had suspicious brown stains on it and a strong odor that alarmed him.

"It didn't seem right, him still being missing and me turning their master bedroom into an office and then those splatters on that picture. Like I got the heebie-jeebies."

Lovato also claimed that he heard a strange sound in the bathtub in the master bathroom. He said that, upon inspection, it looked about the same color and consistency as the stains on the mattress and carpet he removed.

The same day he moved the allegedly bloodstained items from the Rudin's bedroom, Margaret Rudin asked Lovato to mail a package addressed to her mother. Lovato claimed that he forgot to mail the package, and ultimately turned it over to the police. After obtaining a search warrant, police opened the package and discovered several personal items inside, including a postcard from Israel signed "Love, Yehuda," a photo of Yehuda Sharon, the man with whom police suspected that Margaret Rudin was having an affair, and a handwritten letter from Rudin to her mother containing the message, "Please hold on to my Ye."

Attorneys discovered later that Lovato reported all these mysterious findings after Ron Rudin's other trustees announced their reward for information about Ron's disappearance. However, Lovato argued that he cooperated with police before anyone told him there was a reward, which Ron's trustees did grant him.

The most suspicious thing that Margaret Rudin did, according to police, was going on the run before the state served her with her indictment. Investigators believed that, if Margaret were innocent, she would not have fled. However, Margaret says that she ran out of fear, not guilt.

"[I ran] because I was afraid of being found by Ron's shadowy business associates... It was difficult. I was always looking over my shoulder. I was always afraid, I was afraid of who stood to gain the most, you know, from Ron's murder."

During the trial, the state also used the testimony of almost 70 witnesses, including Yehuda Sharon and Margaret's sister, Donna Cantrell. Prosecutors granted Yehuda Sharon total immunity in exchange for his testimony against Margaret Rudin. However, when he took the stand, he not only had little to say regarding Margaret's guilt, he denied aiding her in disposing of Ron Rudin's remains. He told the court that he rented a van, planning to make a trip from Vegas to California for his business on the night in question. However, he said that he only made it half way there and then turned around due to unexpected weather conditions. Furthermore, his destination was the opposite direction from the place where officials found Ron Rudin's remains. Once the prosecution determined that Margaret's friend, Yehuda Sharon, was likely not an accomplice to Ron's murder, no other suspects were detained or questions, and most people assumed that Margaret had somehow dismembered her husband's body, put it in the heavy steamer trunk and hauled it out to the desert all by herself.

Cantrell testified that she was aware of her sister's marital problems. She said that Margaret had spoken to her many times about Ron's drinking and her suspicions about his involvement with other women. She made comments on Rudin's restless desire to get away from Ron.

"I said, 'I thought you were going to divorce him,' and she said, 'He's not in very good health. He can't even walk without being out of breath, and I think I'll wait.' [Margaret told me] to tell [police] that she and Ron were getting along better than ever. And that the girlfriend wasn't an issue. [I don't] think that this statement would have been true."

Despite the authorities' strong belief that she murdered her husband, Margaret Rudin maintained her innocents. In interviews after the trial and her conviction, she states repeatedly that she loved her husband and could never kill him. She suggested that there might be another motive for her husband's murder.

"Nobody knows the whole Ron. That's the part that worries me. Maybe there's something that was going on with a business or a personal deal."

Margaret also suspected that someone knew more than they told detectives.

"I think that there are people that know things. I think that there are people who haven't come forth before. Maybe they didn't know how, maybe they were afraid, maybe they were intimidated."

Margaret Rudin's trial was rocky from the beginning. One of her defense attorneys, Michael Amador, started with an opening statement, which consisted of nothing but a long, irrelevant, self-based speech.

"This is a great day, in a lot of different ways. Some days are difficult; some days we hear bad news or we go through a difficult time, but every day, every day, depending on how you look at it, with a few exceptions, can be a celebration.

This is a great today for me. This is a culmination of a career. The people in this case, we are not strangers; we know each other. Chris and I were sworn in as deputy DAs the same day. And I congratulate Chris on a presentation that was organized and well thought out, the best money can buy. It was really good.

If you want to know an opinion about me, I guarantee you'll find some, different ones from different people. Not many people know me. I have few close friends, like Ronald Rudin had few close friends.

I could be a wonderful, caring father, coaching soccer, helping kids with their homework, which I did the first time I got married when they were young.

Then another day, I might scream at someone, yell at them for-I don't know-for asking me some question, because I was too busy and I was thinking of something else.

The difficulty I have at times is communicating to people. I have to look at it and talk to other people and they will bring me back down to earth and say, Mike, what are you trying to say? What are you trying to get across?"

Amador also made a strange, challenging statement.

"During the course of the trial, there may be objections and things like that. Don't worry about it."

Judge Joseph Bonaventure cut off Amador's speech.

"I don't know what that means: Don't worry about objections. We have to do other things. I have no idea what that means. If there's an objection, I'm either going to overrule it or sustain it and that's the law...

I keep saying this-and I let you get away with a lot, Mr. Amador-but the purpose for an opening statement is just to indicate what the evidence is going to tend to show and not go into your personal beliefs and your passion and soccer dad and yelling at the staff and whether you were a green lawyer and know all the cops and used to be a D.A. and you communicate differently. I never heard that in [an] opening statement in my life."

During the opening statements, the State quoted a portion of Margaret Rudin's diary.

"My life has always been unique, exciting, full of change, challenges and stimulus and full of interesting casts of characters and that is okay.

It just is, and I accept that for my past, but I know that, by programming my mind, I can now redirect any future stage plays and pick my own screen play and cast, because I am the producer, director and star of any and all new plays on my stage called life.

I've always vaguely known these facts and lived my life accordingly, but I never realized what control-I never realized what control I could have over every segment of this one time stage production called "Margaret's Life.""

Amador did a curious thing at the trial. He employed a makeup artist from a professional modeling agency and paid almost $500 an hour, out of his own pocket, to make Margaret appear worn, delicate, and tired.

Amador got under Judge Bonaventure's skin by repeatedly being late to appear in court, questionable forms he submitted, and his cell phone, which he never turned off or down during the trial. Rumors eventually spread that Amador was using drugs, drinking and partying all night long when he had to be in court early the next morning.

Rumors circulated that Amador was also behaving inappropriately with Margaret Rudin's belongings and private, confidential information. Amador hired a new office assistant named Annie Jackson during the proceedings for the Rudin trial. She revealed information regarding some of the rumors about Amador.

"There is no other way to say the following: when Mr. Amador told the court that he did not have any book or movie contracts, he was lying. Michael Amador does have book contracts and movie contracts regarding the Margaret Rudin case. When we returned to the office after Mr. Amador made those false representations to the court, he asked me to grab all of the contracts so that he could put them in his little safe in the back closet. He told me, "I don't want anyone to find out that I have these, then I'm sure they'll be investigating and looking for these.""

Margaret asked early on for an even amount of participation from her attorneys. She asked that Thomas Pitaro take a more active role in the proceedings, because she did not believe that Michael Amador was properly prepared.

"We haven't even subpoenaed my witnesses yet. And I'm getting so nervous. I mean, I'm getting panicky."

Pitaro agreed after warning the judge that, although he would do his best, he was uncertain if he would be able to uphold that bargain throughout the entire trial.

Throughout all the chaos in the Rudin trial, one juror believed Margaret's side of the story. During the first couple of days of deliberation, she held fast to her opinion that Margaret did not kill Ron. However, hours before the foreperson read the jury's verdict, juror #11 changed her vote. She was distraught, wiping her eyes with a napkin. She hesitated before replying with a hushed "Yes" when the court asked her if the verdict was, in fact, hers, too.

Even though the verdict was ultimately unanimous, the juror cried as she apologized to Rudin when the foreperson read the jury's verdict.

During the time before she opted to vote Margaret Rudin guilty, juror #11 faced allegations from her peers of choosing not to join the deliberation efforts, lying, and calling one of the jury substitutes with her concerns about the case. Amador said he thought the juror was possibly "brow-beaten" into changing her vote.

Foreperson for the Rudin case's jury, Ronald Vest, said that no one "twisted her arm."

"We didn't bribe her or threaten her. She came to this on her own."

Vest believed that Rudin's was an open and shut case.

"Rudin's guilt was clear early on. [The defense's case was] a waste of time... [Amador was] bordering on incompetent... [The guilty verdict was a] slam dunk with a stepladder... I didn't buy any of it. I don't think any of us bought any of the defense case. The mountain of evidence had 11 of the jurors ready to convict as early as Thursday, but one person from the beginning did not see it that way... juror #11 seemed so bent on acquitting Rudin that [I] began to wonder if she had been bribed or threatened or simply wanted attention. [I] confronted her about [my] suspicions, and she denied them. There was a little bit of swearing. It was fast and furious but we hashed it out."

Vest admitted that he had had to request substitutes on a few occasions, because his special needs students were struggling in class without him. He believed that, had he not been there, they would not have been able to replace him.

"Six substitutes, three of which said they would never come back and one who just sat at the desk shaking like he was scared... my principal said, Well, maybe there's some reason why you need to be on this jury."

The judge in the Rudin trial met with the hesitant juror privately, in his chambers, to address her contact, and discussion about case-related information, with an alternate juror. Whenever Margaret Rudin's defense team broached the subject, the court dismissed it, stating that it had little impact on the outcome of the trial.

Margaret Rudin's conviction shocked Amador. He spoke with disdain about the prosecutors. He could not believe that the prosecutors successfully sold their case.

"If you have any understanding of psychology, history, or criminology, women don't do that, men do," said Amador. "That kind of mutilation is done by men over money or, in rare cases, serial killers. Women don't even order stuff like that—they want it clean... [The prosecutors] make me sick... I don't know how it is that right-thinking people can find someone guilty with no evidence."

Rudin had requested a mistrial due to Amador's antics and all the dissention with the jury. Pitaro led the defense team at the motion, hoping to prove that Amador was ill prepared for the case and not behaving with appropriate competence as an attorney.

"The fundamental problem that we have is this case is not ready to go to trial. For whatever reason it's not ready, it's not ready. That's obvious to any observer of this case, that for the first two weeks this is not the way you try cases and this is not the way you try murder cases. And what we are putting on in front of the world is a farce, and that disturbs me as an attorney. [T]his has become a sham, a farce and a mockery."

The State expressed similar concerns.

"Already we have an appellate issue now, should they have hired a forensic accountant. And I mean they came into this thing hiring their experts two weeks before the trial and they didn't start looking at the evidence until the day of trial. Two days into it, we still don't have reports back for most of them... Mr. Pitaro is coming in now, he's going to try to read the stuff and catch up. He already feels there's certain things that should have happened that didn't happen. All I can say is we're really uncomfortable with the record here."

The district court, however, was hesitant to declare a mistrial because of the double jeopardy laws. As it turned out, those did not apply in Margaret Rudin's case.

Amador stood with Margaret Rudin and the rest of her defense team during the motion for mistrial. However, when the prosecutors submitted documentation regarding his ineffectiveness, he contradicted himself.

"Nobody worked harder or spent more time before or during the Rudin trial nor knew the case better than I... [I] spend many hours on the case, from the time [I] took it in August of 2000 and [my] vacation in November 2000... [I] filed at least 24 motions and investigated all major witnesses in the case and organized their files prior to the vacation."

The defense also argued that improper communication took place between the judge, juror 11 and the alternate, which tainted the jury. According to the alternate, juror 11 called the alternate, saying she was upset because she was the only person in favor of a not guilty verdict and because she had gotten into an altercation with the staff person at a restaurant during a recess. After questioning the alternate and the juror in the presence of the State and the defense, the district court denied Rudin's motion for a mistrial. The district court also chose not to replace the juror. They concluded that neither the jury nor Rudin's case were compromised.

The court removed Amador from Margaret Rudin's case, but rejected her request for a mistrial. The judge almost immediately disregarded Margaret's mistrial motion.

"[Rudin] failed to present any specific argument to support a determination that she has been prejudiced. [The] affidavits are legally insufficient, as conclusions, rumors, beliefs, and opinions are not sufficient to form a basis for a new trial... As to Mr. Amador's personal antics which the defense seems to harp upon as tantalizing tidbits, this court feels it is not honorable to kick a man when he is down as the record speaks for itself. Rudin, at taxpayer expense, also had at her side criminal defense attorneys Thomas Pitaro and John Momot."

Bonaventure was biased, blunt, and cold at Margaret's sentencing hearing, just as he was throughout the entire trial.

"You're going to be locked away in the cold confines of your prison cell, never to be heard from again."

Although she received life in a medium security facility, plus a year for planting the bugs in her husband's office, they also added that she would be eligible for parole in 2011. She began preparing, and petitioning, for her appeal, carefully heeding the filing deadlines.

The appeals court believed that one of Margaret Rudin's former attorneys, Dayvid Figler, was responsible for her initial petitions for appeal. Figler denied any wrongdoing, and said that, although he was not at fault, she did deserve a shot at a new trial.

"I didn't screw up her trial. I didn't screw up her appeal. The court was giving extra time to get this very burdensome case before it. Everyone was operating under the assumption that she had more time to file the post-conviction appeal."

Figler called Rudin's appeal a "very complicated, burdensome, voluminous case" and said that after he took it on, the trial judge granted him extra time because the case was so complex.

Christopher Oram, the lawyer who represented Margaret Rudin during her recent appeal for a new trial, was thrilled with the opportunity.

"She is absolutely innocent. We've been working to prove it for a long time. I'm trying to reverse 10 years of complex litigation that was very unfair... I believe in her innocence. I'm ready to fight, and I wish they would stop playing their games. In the end, get in the ring and fight."

The Ninth Circuit Court of Appeals said that a technicality should not hinder Margaret Rudin's attempt to prove that a lawyer at her original trial ineffectually proved her case. Judge Mary Murguia believed that Figler did not serve Margaret to the best of his ability.

"While Figler regularly attended the court's status hearings, he appears to have done nothing else in support of his client's request for post-conviction relief. [Figler had the case for 645 days] and during that time, [he] had filed nothing in either state or federal court."

In 2007, Oram filed the first and only petition for post-conviction relief, according to Murguia.

Sally Loehrer, a district judge, ruled in 2008 that Michael Amador's performance did constitute as ineffectual in her original trial, and as a result, Margaret Rudin was entitled to a new trial.

"[It was a] case laced with intrigue and spins and loops involving a cast of characters and witnesses [that seemed to have] a lot of ulterior motives."

However, two years later, the Supreme Court overruled, stating that there was not enough evidence to sustain the order.

The Ninth Circuit Court reviewed all the evidence from the original trial, as well as Margaret Rudin's complaints, and her defense team's strategies. They do not believe that all defense attorneys adequately represent their clients just because they participate in every aspect of the trial. They made mention of evidence that was not previously mentioned.

"Sometime during the trial, the defense team located the person who sold the trunk to Rudin and established that it was not a large humpback trunk, but one that was much too small to fit a corpse inside. The defense also located Barbara Orcutt, who indicated that Rudin was indeed concerned about Ron's disappearance and had asked her right after his disappearance to organize a search in the Mt. Charleston area, where she believed Ron might have been. The State apparently had this information, but did not share it with the defense. It is unrealistic to think that the jurors could have put out of their minds all the evidence and adverse events, including the continual admonishment of defense counsel by the district court judge; the bizarre opening statement; the constant continuances and delays throughout the trial, which I am sure were held against the defense; and the belated presentation of important evidence. These harmful events resulted from Amador's conflict of interest and lack of preparation and now require reversal of this case... The evidence certainly indicated that Amador secured media rights while representing Rudin, which was a violation of the Nevada Rules of Professional Conduct.9...Amador was clearly more interested in obtaining information for his book and getting media attention than in developing Rudin's defense."

They also noted the testimony from Annie Jackson, Amador's assistant, and found new information there, as well. Jackson claimed that Amador did not turn over several of Rudin's files, containing diaries, witness statements, and pictures, to the public defender's office because he thought he might need the information in the future.

"I believe there is sufficient evidence in the record, without the necessity of post-trial proceedings, to establish that the defense was totally unprepared to try this case and that Amador had a substantial conflict of interest with his client. This was prejudicial to Rudin, and the result reached was unreliable."

Margaret appeals to the public in a letter she wrote from the Florence McClure Women's Correctional Center.

"The new trial I won [on] March 10, 2015, in the Ninth Circuit Court of Appeals has been blocked by the new NV Attorney General. Next week, their writ to the U.S. Supreme court will be filed."

She explains that, if her case lands in the 99% that skip review this session, it will return to the Ninth Circuit. Since they have already voted in her favor before, she hopes that once again, the NCCA will find her worthy of a new trial, and that this time their decision will be permanent. She maintains her innocence, and she continues to push for her appeal, and her opportunity to have her side of the story told.

HUSBAND KILLER : THE TRUE STORY OF MICHELLE HALL

105

TORI BAKER

It's never easy being a member of a blended family. There's a certain understanding that comes along with a second or third marriage – especially one involving children – that there is going to be a fundamental need for combined effort, tolerance and compromise.

When Michelle Garner remarried for what would be the third and last time, family and friends believed she had finally found happiness after reconnecting with an old high-school flame.

John Brittson "Britt" Hall, an aircraft mechanic and home builder, had known his own fair share of heartache; he was recently divorced when he found his old high school girlfriend, Michelle, on an online dating web site.

Britt Hall and Michelle Garner first met in 1986 while attending high school in Newnan, GA. The two briefly dated before Michelle Hall graduated in 1987.

"They both were in the popular clique," forensic psychologist Robert Brion said. "Britt was a baseball player that all of the girls had a crush on. Michelle was popular herself, very outgoing with a lot of friends."

The parents of Britt and Michelle were friends as well but they didn't consider the dating relationship between Michelle and Britt to be a serious one. After graduation, Michelle would move away and she would marry a man named Rusty Hart. The couple would have two daughters until their divorce in 1996.

The single mom worked as a dental assistant to support her daughters. Times were tight until 1999 when she met and married Steve Davis.

"Steve Davis was a businessman," Brion said. "He was divorced himself with a daughter of his own. He met Michelle and quickly fell for her charms as she could come across as a very warm and caring person. He asked her to marry him after about a year of dating."

Michelle would become pregnant during the union and give birth to her third daughter, Alyssa.

Unfortunately, her second marriage met the same fate as her first and within a few years, the couple had filed for divorce, citing irreconcilable differences.

Britt did well for himself after high school, becoming an airline mechanic for Delta Airlines. He made good money with Delta until they laid him off. He then went into business with his father in home construction until ultimately returning back to Delta after they had a rehire.

His marriage started to fail, however. His first wife cited that Britt had "mental problems" and filed for divorce, stating that the marriage was "irretrievably broken."

"Britt's first wife would take him to court at least six to eight times a year after their divorce," Brion said. "He was depressed and the court visits weren't helping."

His divorce would coincide with Michelle's impending divorce with Steve Davis. Her divorce with Davis was a particularly nasty one and Britt could sympathize. They would reconnect over a dating website.

In the midst of her own divorce, Garner was happy to find love again with Britt Hall as they rekindled old flames. Shortly after reconnecting, Britt invited Michelle over for Sunday lunch with his family, and all seemed well for the couple.

"Michelle did mention to Britt's family that she was going through some difficult times with her divorce," Brion said. "She was cheerful throughout but hinted that the custody battles she was going through were quite serious."

Little did Britt Hall's family know that their excitement would soon be turned to devastation; a tragedy that would make national headlines and be detailed in various murder documentaries.

THE BRADY BUNCH

Ronald Hall, Britt's father was all to happy to have Michelle back in his son's life. At least at first.

"We visited and talked," Ronald said. "And she came in and was just as happy as she ever was," he said.

It wasn't long before Britt Hall's romance with Garner turned more serious, and the two tied the knot in September of 2006. The new marriage was an adjustment, to say the least. Britt had three children from his previous marriage and Michelle Hall had three of her own children as well. The blended family of eight was now living in Britt Hall's town home.

"You can imagine how tight the living quarters were," Brion said. "But Michelle's girls really took to their new stepfather. They became comfortable enough to call him 'Dad'."

Britt wanted a bigger home and decided to build a large home with the help of his father. The men paid for contractors to pour concrete and establish the foundation, but father and son built the majority of the house by hand.

"People didn't know where the couple were getting the money to build the house," Brion said. "But Britt did most of the work himself after the foundation was laid. So he was able to save a lot of money when it came to sweat equity. That's a testimony to how badly he wanted the marriage between he and Michelle to work out."

When all was said and done, Britt and Michelle Hall were the proud owners of a beautiful 4100 square foot home on ten acres, the perfect place to spend the rest of their lives together. The brand new house boasted vaulted ceilings, granite counter tops, and a finished basement. The construction would prove to be a house of cards, however, as things were brewing underneath the surface.

Michelle didn't have much luck with her two previous marriages, and although individual accounts may vary, her two former husbands are both to have reported being abused by Michelle during the course of their marriage.

Michelle never had a firm grasp on her emotions and didn't handle anger well. These character flaws would not bode well for her life with

Britt. Dealing with both partners' ex-spousal issues including custody and visitation, Michelle and Britt found themselves tinkering on the edge of divorce after a few months into their marriage.

"The way Britt and Michelle handled their issues were different," said family friend Sue Mathis. "Michelle was quicker to speak her mind and a lot of times, Britt just wanted her to try to gain a little bit more self-control."

Dealing with his own ex-wife and their similar divorce problems, Britt Hall was also facing his own internal battles with depression. Although he wasn't often the instigator in their frequent arguments, he was known to fervently engage in the verbal conflicts. While this certainly wasn't conducive to a happy and fruitful marriage, Britt Hall made it clear to friends he would not give up on his family and the life he had built.

The next couple of years came with continued stress, intensified by financial worries after the Halls realized they had gotten too far deep in debt as a result of building their dream home. Notices of foreclosure, liens on the house, and over-extensions were haunting the couple and causing both spouses to hit a breaking point.

On July 30, 2008, it was another typical tense day in the Hall household. Friends say Britt Hall, already aggravated due to a landscaper failing to complete a job on time, went to the store to pick-up hot dogs for a family get-together.

"Hey hon," Britt said as he called his wife. "How many hot dogs do you think I should get-"

"Count how many damn people are here," Michelle snapped. "That's how much you should get."

This would be the snide comeback that would break the straw in Britt's back. He grew tired at her constant bickering and baiting. When he came home that evening, a fight would ensue.

Michelle's youngest daughter, Alyssa, was in the living room watching television as her mother vacuumed to prepare for the company soon arriving. When Britt Hall told Alyssa to turn the TV down, another argument between the couple ensued and Hall immediately told her daughter to go upstairs to her bedroom and not come out until she was called.

There are only two individuals who know the details of what followed on that evening, and only one of them lived to tell. When all was said and done, Britt would be dead and Michelle would be charged with murder.

The 911 call came in at 8:02 p.m. by a frantic Michelle who told dispatchers that her husband had tried to kill her and commit suicide.

"He shot at me, and we were fighting to get it," Michelle told dispatchers regarding the weapon. She said she heard the gun go off twice. Seconds later, she told dispatchers her husband was turning blue.

When police arrived, Britt Hall was dead and had three noticeable gunshot wounds to his body: one on his left arm, one on his right thigh, and a close-range shot to his chest. Michelle Hall, bruised, scraped and covered in blood, told first responders the same story she had told dispatchers: her suicidal husband had tried to kill her before turning the gun on himself.

Prior to further investigation, deputies on the scene immediately called Britt Hall's parents and told them their son had committed suicide. The Halls refused to believe the news.

"Things just seemed to be going too good at this time in his life for him to have done that," said his mother, Charlene Hall. "I knew he didn't kill himself; I knew for a fact that didn't happen."

It didn't take long for police to begin seeing the crime scene a little differently than Michelle had described. Blood splatter and numerous bullet holes covered the downstairs bedroom, and a trail of blood led into the bathroom where Britt Hall's lifeless body now lay. If this was a suicide, there sure was a struggle beforehand.

Investigators gave Michelle the opportunity to explain the scene. She told how an argument between the couple turned violent when

Britt Hall threw her onto the bed. He immediately went into the study and she followed him.

Then she noticed the gun on the computer desk.

Knowing her husband was battling depression, she said she immediately became concerned with his safety, worried that he may use the gun to harm himself.

Michelle stated that she instinctively dove for the gun, and that's when Britt Hall reached for it as well and the two began struggling for possession.

After both Michelle and her husband lost control of he gun, she quickly picked up the weapon and began shooting rounds into the walls and floor in an effort to unload the gun.

In the hall, Britt Hall caught up with her and that's when she said he threatened to kill her. In yet another entanglement of an attempt for control of the gun, Michelle said the gun accidentally went off. This shot punctured Britt Hall's thigh, and that's when Hall claimed she went to call for help.

Britt Hall began crawling into the bathroom, unable to walk and calling out her name for help. When she approached him, gun in hand, she said he grabbed the pistol from her, put it to his chest, and pulled the trigger.

The problem with her story, however, was that most suicides don't entail multiple gunshot wounds. Additionally, the manner in which the fatal shot was delivered raised eyebrows for investigators.

"I've worked many suicides in my career, and I've never worked a suicide that I can remember where a man had shot himself in the chest," Lt John Lewis said.

Furthermore, the gunshot wound on Britt Hall's chest had no signs of charring or burning around the entry wound, signs which usually indicate a self-inflicted wound.

Britt Hall also had a shattered elbow and a bullet hole in his left arm. Three different shots, all which led investigators to believe they weren't being told the whole story.

Michelle did her best to persuade the investigative team to believe her story, but her story changed upon being brought to the station for questioning. While at first she claimed the two struggled for control over the gun, she then claimed Britt Hall was never actually in possession of the gun at all.

Coupled with the evidence at the crime scene and her story's inconsistencies, Michelle was charged the next morning with the murder of her husband.

Crucial to the prosecution's case was the testimony of Michelle's youngest daughter, Alyssa, who was in the home during the shooting. Police brought the 8-year-old in for questioning immediately following the incident and she clearly stated she heard her step-father pleading with her mother to "put the gun down," she said. Alyssa would ultimately testify in her mother's trial in 2009.

Facing charges of malice murder and aggravated assault, Michelle vehemently denied killing her husband. She insisted that he died of a self-inflicted gunshot wound after threatening suicide and fighting with her over the .38 caliber revolver.

The fight that evening was par for the course, she said. The two regularly got into verbal and physical altercations, and their marriage was falling apart due to financial stress. They would also constantly fight over ex-spouses, custody and visitation regarding the six children. Although there were no police reports relating to any domestic altercations in the home before, family and friends knew things weren't okay on the home front.

"Britt would spend several nights driving to work calling me and saying 'I don't know what to do.' He would have done everything in his power to save his marriage, even if it was not worth saving. He was terrified of failure," said Mathis.

One of the first fights that turned physical in front of the family was in November 2006, when Britt Hall's eldest daughter came into the room to find Michelle Hall unconscious. Her father quickly ushered her out of the room and told her not to worry about it. The next couple of years only brought more trouble due to the same old problems and Britt's alleged mental illness.

Britt was prescribed three different types of medication for depression at the time of his death, police confirmed.

But the physical evidence did not add up to suicide. Initially, the Georgia Bureau of Investigation estimated the fatal gunshot to have been fired from around 18-24 inches away. This is not consistent with suicide, detectives argued. While many victims of mental illness fall prey to suicide each year, the facts must add up. In this case, they did not.

If convicted, Michelle was facing life in prison.

In September of 2009, testimonies were heard by Alyssa Davis, as well as responding officers Capt. Tony Grant and Sgt. Freddy Cox, about what they saw and heard on the night of the shooting.

Cox testified that Hall's appearance was "consistent with someone who'd been in a physical altercation" and that Hall had bruises, scrapes and blood on her neck and forehead as well as blood on her hands and a knot on her elbow.

During his testimony, Grant stated he immediately noticed that Hall's face was red and she had what appeared to be gun-shot residue on her hand, even though she was stating her husband had committed suicide.

There were multiple bullet holes throughout the downstairs of the home when police arrived on the scene, Grant testified. Two bullets were recovered from Britt Hall's body and three more were found in the house.

Grant said a blood pattern analysis showed blood spatters of 90 degrees in the downstairs quarters outside of the bathroom, proof that Britt Hall crawled into the bathroom after being wounded.

Defense Attorney Mike Kam said that while in no uncertain terms would he call the key ear witness a liar, her age and her location during the shooting did not make for the most reliable testimony.

"She was eight; she didn't see anything, she clearly got some of the facts confused." Kam said in an interview. "She's not someone who is used to being asked questions in formal interview settings. Who knows what she remembered, or what happened?"

Additionally, Kam indicated that Michelle certainly didn't fit the description of a murderer. Outside of two divorces, Hall had no criminal record. She was law-abiding citizen, with nothing in her background which would give the assumption she was capable of murder, he said.

But the jury had heard enough. On September 25, 2009, Michelle Hall was found guilty on all counts in the death of her husband Britt.

Not long after her conviction, Hall's attorneys filed a motion for a new trial, citing trial court errors. Coweta County Superior Court Judge Jack Kirby denied the motion and the defense attorneys took the case to the Supreme Court.

On September 22, 2010, the Supreme Court of Georgia upheld the conviction, despite Hall's defense's argument that the trial court erred by admitting similar transaction evidence and prior consistent statements.

Hall's defense stated that testimony from both of her ex-husbands that she was verbally and physically abusive were inadmissible because they were not "sufficiently similar" to establish proof of the crimes for which she was charged, according to the opinion of the Supreme Court. It also stated that "in cases of domestic violence, prior incidents of abuse against family members or sexual partners are more generally permitted because there is a logical connection between violent acts against two different persons with whom the accused had a similar emotional or intimate attachment."

The opinion also added that the fifteen and thirteen-year lapses of time between her ex-husband's allegations of abuse to the alleged shooting of her husband did not require exclusion of evidence.

"Given that the similar transaction evidence reflects appellant's behavior towards prior spouses, we conclude that any prejudice from the age of these prior incidents was outweighed by the probative value of the evidence under the particular facts of this case and the purpose for which the similar transactions were offered."

Eighteen months later, however, Michelle retained a new attorney who filed a habeas corpus petition, stating Michelle was given ineffective legal counsel by Kam during her trial in 2009. Senior Judge Robert B. Struble presided over the hearing and determined that Hall was in-fact entitled to a new trial. Struble agreed that Kam, Hall's trial attorney, was "ineffective and fell below the minimum guarantee of representation under the constitution," a press release said.

While Michelle may have been looking forward to another chance at redemption, The Attorney General's Office quickly announced their plans to appeal the habeas corpus ruling to the Georgia Supreme Court.

In a press release on March 30, 2012, Coweta County District Attorney Peter John Skandalakis expressed his respectful disapproval of the court's ruling and that in stating Kam was ineffective for representation, "the court erroneously applied the wrong standard under the law."

Skandalakis said he was optimistic that the Supreme Court will conclude that Hall had a legally sufficient defense and that her conviction would be upheld after review of the appeal.

On January 22, 2013, the Supreme Court found Hall's convictions to be fair and just, denying insufficient representation during her 2009 trial. According to the court summary, the Supreme Court concluded that the habeas corpus petition did not conduct proper legal analysis to determine the effectiveness of Hall's defense.

The opinion references Strickland v. Washington, a 1984 Supreme Court case in which it determined that to be granted a new trial, a defendant must show that it was due to insufficient performance by defense that the defendant was found guilty.

Michelle's argument for her habeas corpus petition was that "if she were in the same room when her young daughter was questioned, she could have assisted her attorney by prompting him with specific information," the court says in its opinion. However, it was determined during the habeas hearing that any information she would have portrayed to her attorney was already known information to both parties. "As such, Hall has failed to show actual prejudice, and her claim of ineffective assistance of counsel should have been rejected," the opinion said.

Today, Michelle Hall remains in a Coweta County prison.

Since her conviction, Michelle's ex-husbands have been given full custody of her three respective daughters.

She won't be eligible for parole until 2039. She will be 70 years old.